OTHER BOOKS BY

ALBERT CAMUS

Awarded the Nobel Prize for Literature in 1957

(The dates given are the dates of publication in America)

NOVELS

The Fall (*La Chute*) 1957
The Plague (*La Peste*) 1948
The Stranger (*L'Étranger*) 1946

SHORT STORIES

Exile and the Kingdom (*L'Exil et le Royaume*) 1958

PLAYS

The Possessed (*Les Possédés*) 1960
Caligula and Three Other Plays: (*Caligula, Le Malentendu, L'État de siège, Les Justes*) The Misunderstanding, State of Siege, The Just Assassins 1958

ESSAYS

The Myth of Sisyphus (*Le Mythe de Sisyphe*) and Other Essays 1955
The Rebel (*L'Homme révolté*) 1954

These are Borzoi Books published in NEW YORK
by ALFRED A. KNOPF

Resistance, Rebellion, and Death : : : : :

Resistance, Rebellion,
and Death

by Albert Camus

Translated from the French and with an Introduction by
JUSTIN O'BRIEN

NEW YORK : ALFRED A. KNOPF : 1961

The essays, originally published in French, were selected from *Lettres à un ami allemand,* copyright 1948 by Librairie Gallimard; *Actuelles,* copyright 1950 by Librairie Gallimard; *Actuelles II,* copyright 1953 by Librairie Gallimard; *Actuelles III,* copyright © 1958 by Librairie Gallimard; *Réflexions sur la peine capitale,* copyright © 1957 by Calmann-Lévy; *Discours de Suède,* copyright © 1958 by Librairie Gallimard. The following were interviews: "Kadar Had His Day of Fear," which appeared as "Kadar a eu son jour de peur" in *Franc-Tireur* in 1957; "Socialism of the Gallows," which appeared as "Le socialisme des potences," and "The Wager of Our Generation," which appeared as "Le pari de notre generation," both in *Demain* in 1957.

L. C. catalog card number: 60–16703

THIS IS A BORZOI BOOK,
PUBLISHED BY ALFRED A. KNOPF, INC.

PUBLISHED FEBRUARY 13, 1961
SECOND PRINTING, MARCH 1961
THIRD PRINTING, JULY 1961

INTRODUCTION

IT WAS as much for the positive stand Albert Camus took on the issues of the day as for his creative writing—or rather it was for the combination of the two—that he was awarded the Nobel Prize in 1957 at the early age of forty-three. Because, in everything he wrote, he spoke to us of our problems and in our language, without raising his voice or indulging in oratory, he illuminated, as the Nobel citation stated, "the problems of the human conscience in our time." Over and above intellectual or political leadership, he provided the moral guidance the postwar generation needed. By remaining flagrantly independent, he could speak out both against the Russian slave-labor camps and against U.S. support of Franco's Spain. By overcoming the immature nihilism and despair that he saw as poisoning our century, he emerged as the staunch defender of our positive moral values and of "those silent men who, throughout the world, endure the life that has been made for them."

Indeed, one of the things that endeared Camus to all of us is that he spoke for all. As he said in the brilliant credo he voiced in the Stockholm town hall upon accepting the most universally distinguished award, ". . . the writer's function is not without ardu-

v

ous duties. By definition, he cannot serve today those who make history; he must serve those who are subject to it." Whether we fight in the regular army or wage war as civilians in the shadows of some maquis, whether we succumb to famine or slink into exile, whether we are crushed by dictators or put to death by due process of law, are we not all "subject to history"?

In France Camus made his mark as a journalist and polemicist at about the same time that he asserted himself as one of that country's leading novelists. But in 1943–4 his readers didn't yet know that the author of the anonymous editorials they were clipping from the clandestine newspaper Combat as the most vigorous expression of their own feelings and the author of L'Etranger were one and the same person. Only after the Liberation of Paris, when Combat came out into the open, did they discover that the forthright, inspiring editorialist they had admired was named Albert Camus.

Little by little, his compatriots learned that this young Algerian Frenchman had begun life as a journalist, that, after having incurred the government's wrath for his most revelatory reportage on the sorry condition of the Kabyle tribes of Algeria, he had come over to Occupied France and helped to found what was both an intelligence network and an underground newspaper. And, as admiration for his first two novels, The Stranger and The Plague, grew in all countries, Camus continued to write essays dealing with the major problems, social and political, that haunted him and his generation. In 1950 he brought out a collected volume of those articles under the title Actuelles; a second volume followed in 1953 and a third in 1958, soon after the Nobel Prize.

In the last year of his life, Albert Camus chose from the three volumes of Actuelles the twenty-three essays he considered most worthy of preservation in English. They deal with the perennially current issues that periodically tore him from his creative writing to speak out, as he said, "in the service of truth and the service of freedom": war and resistance in a Europe dominated by prisons, executions, and exile; the tragedies of Algeria and of Hungary; the horror of the death penalty; and the writer's commitment.

The very title Actuelles, which unfortunately could not be carried over into English, is typical of the man— concise without being precise, allusive without being descriptive, and modest. Indeed, this mere adjective in the feminine plural meaning "current," "prevailing," or "of present interest" almost requires a gloss in the original. What noun did Camus suppress for greater ambiguity— pensées, réflexions, vues?

To some readers these essays will introduce an utterly new Camus—what one might be tempted to call the Camus actuel. But he wrote them concurrently with his novels and plays and in them explored the same *themes he touched upon in his creative work. An essential part of the man and the writer, these occasional articles and speeches reveal more clearly the position of one of the most lucid spirits of our time—one who was both committed and aloof, or, as he himself implied in his moral tale "The Artist at Work," at once solidary and solitary.*

And Camus would never have allowed anyone to consider these essays as incidental to, or less important than, his plays and novels, for he recognized them as a significant part of that opera omnia *with which he now —too soon, alas—must face posterity.*

JUSTIN O'BRIEN

CONTENTS

LETTERS TO A GERMAN FRIEND   1

THE LIBERATION OF PARIS   33
THE BLOOD OF FREEDOM   35
THE NIGHT OF TRUTH   38

THE FLESH   41

PESSIMISM AND TYRANNY   55
PESSIMISM AND COURAGE   57
DEFENSE OF INTELLIGENCE   61

THE UNBELIEVER AND CHRISTIANS   67

WHY SPAIN?   75

DEFENSE OF FREEDOM   85
BREAD AND FREEDOM   87
HOMAGE TO AN EXILE   98

ALGERIA   109
PREFACE TO ALGERIAN REPORTS   111
LETTER TO AN ALGERIAN MILITANT   126
APPEAL FOR A CIVILIAN TRUCE   131
ALGERIA 1958   143

HUNGARY 155
    Kadar Had His Day of Fear 157
    Socialism of the Gallows 165

REFLECTIONS ON THE GUILLOTINE 173

THE ARTIST AND HIS TIME 235
    The Wager of Our Generation 237
    Create Dangerously 249

LETTERS TO
A GERMAN FRIEND

for

RENÉ LEYNAUD

A man does not show his
greatness by being at one extremity, but rather by touch-
ing both at once.

PASCAL

PREFACE
FOR THE ITALIAN EDITION

THE *Letters to a German Friend* [1] were published in France after the Liberation in a limited edition and have never been reprinted. I have always been opposed to their circulation abroad for the reasons that I shall give.

This is the first time they have appeared outside of France and I should not have made up my mind to this had it not been for my long-standing desire to contribute, insofar as I can, to removing the stupid frontiers separating our two territories.

But I cannot let these pages be reprinted without saying what they are. They were written and published clandestinely during the Occupation. They had a purpose, which was to throw some light on the blind battle we were then waging and thereby to make our battle more effective. They are topical writings and hence they may appear unjust. Indeed, if one were to write about defeated Germany, a rather different tone would be called for. But I should simply like to forestall a mis-

[1] The first of these letters appeared in the second issue of the *Revue Libre* in 1943; the second, in No. 3 of the *Cahiers de Libération* in the beginning of 1944. The two others, written for the *Revue Libre,* remained unpublished.

understanding. When the author of these letters says "you," he means not "you Germans" but "you Nazis." When he says "we," this signifies not always "we Frenchmen" but sometimes "we free Europeans." I am contrasting two attitudes, not two nations, even if, at a certain moment in history, these two nations personified two enemy attitudes. To repeat a remark that is not mine, I love my country too much to be a nationalist. And I know that neither France nor Italy would lose anything—quite the contrary—if they both had broader horizons. But we are still wide of the mark, and Europe is still torn. This is why I should be ashamed today if I implied that a French writer could be the enemy of a single nation. I loathe none but executioners. Any reader who reads the *Letters to a German Friend* in this perspective—in other words, as a document emerging from the struggle against violence—will see how I can say that I don't disown a single word I have written here.

FIRST LETTER

You said to me: "The greatness of my country is beyond price. Anything is good that contributes to its greatness. And in a world where everything has lost its meaning, those who, like us young Germans, are lucky enough to find a meaning in the destiny of our nation must sacrifice everything else." I loved you then, but at that point we diverged. "No," I told you, "I cannot believe that everything must be subordinated to a single end. There are means that cannot be excused. And I should like to be able to love my country and still love justice. I don't want just any greatness for it, particularly a greatness born of blood and falsehood. I want to keep it alive by keeping justice alive." You retorted: "Well, you don't love your country."

That was five years ago; we have been separated since then and I can say that not a single day has passed during those long years (so brief, so dazzlingly swift for you!) without my remembering your remark. "You don't love your country!" When I think of your words today, I feel a choking sensation. No, I didn't love my country, if pointing out what is unjust in what we love amounts to not loving, if insisting that what we love should measure up to the finest image we have of her amounts to not loving. That was five years ago, and many men in France thought as I did. Some of them, however, have already been stood up against the wall facing the twelve little black eyes of German destiny. And those men, who in your opinion did not love their country, did more for it than you will ever do for yours, even if it were possible for you to give your life a hundred times. For their heroism was that they had to conquer themselves first. But I am speaking here of two kinds of greatness and of a contradiction about which I must enlighten you.

We shall meet soon again—if possible. But our friendship will be over. You will be full of your defeat. You will not be ashamed of your former victory. Rather, you will longingly remember it with all your crushed might. Today I am still close to you in spirit—your enemy, to be sure, but still a little your friend because I am withholding nothing from you here. Tomorrow all will be over. What your victory could not penetrate, your defeat will bring to an end. But at least, before we become indifferent to each other, I want to leave you a clear idea of what neither peace nor war has taught you to see in the destiny of my country.

I want to tell you at once what sort of greatness keeps us going. But this amounts to telling you what kind of courage we applaud, which is not your kind. For it is not much to be able to do violence when you have been simply preparing for it for years and when violence is more natural to you than thinking. It is a great deal, on the other hand, to face torture and death when you know for a fact that hatred and violence are empty things in themselves. It is a great deal to fight while despising war, to accept losing everything while still preferring happiness, to face destruction while cherishing the idea of a higher civilization. That is how we do more than you because we have to draw on ourselves. You had nothing to conquer in your heart or in your intelligence. We had two enemies, and a military victory was not enough for us, as it was for you who had nothing to overcome.

We had much to overcome—and, first of all, the constant temptation to emulate you. For there is always something in us that yields to instinct, to contempt for intelligence, to the cult of efficiency. Our great virtues eventually become tiresome to us. We become ashamed of our intelligence, and sometimes we imagine some barbarous state where truth would be effortless. But the cure for this is easy; you are there to show us what such imagining would lead to, and we mend our ways. If I believed in some fatalism in history, I should suppose that you are placed beside us, helots of the intelligence, as our living reproof. Then we reawaken to the mind and we are more at ease.

But we also had to overcome the suspicion we had of heroism. I know, you think that heroism is alien to us. You are wrong. It's just that we profess heroism and we distrust it at the same time. We profess it because ten centuries of history have given us knowledge of all that is noble. We distrust it because ten centuries of intelligence have taught us the art and blessings of being natural. In order to face up to you, we had first to be at death's door. And this is why we fell behind all of Europe, which wallowed in falsehood the moment it was necessary, while we were concerned with seeking truth. This is why we were defeated in the beginning: because we were so concerned, while you were falling upon us, to determine in our hearts whether right was on our side.

We had to overcome our weakness for mankind, the image we had formed of a peaceful destiny, that deep-rooted conviction of ours that no victory ever pays, whereas any mutilation of mankind is irrevocable. We had to give up all at once our knowledge and our hope, the reasons we had for loving and the loathing we had for all war. To put it in a word that I suppose you will understand when it comes from me whom you counted as a friend, we had to stifle our passion for friendship.

Now we have done that. We had to make a long detour, and we are far behind. It is a detour that regard for truth imposes on intelligence, that regard for friendship imposes on the heart. It is a detour that safeguarded justice and put truth on the side of those who questioned themselves. And, without a doubt, we paid very dearly for it. We paid for it with humiliations and silences, with bitter experiences, with prison sentences, with executions at dawn, with desertions and separations, with daily pangs of hunger, with emaciated children, and, above all, with humiliation of our human dignity. But that was natural. It took us all that time to find out if we had the right to kill men, if we were allowed to add to the frightful misery of this world. And because of that time lost and recaptured, our defeat accepted and surmounted, those scruples paid for with blood, we French have the right to think today that we entered this war with hands clean—clean as victims and the condemned are—and that we are going to come out of it with hands clean—but clean this time with a great victory won against injustice and against ourselves.

For we shall be victorious, you may be sure. But we shall be victorious thanks to that very defeat, to that long, slow progress during which we found our justification, to that suffering which, in all its injustice, taught us a lesson. It taught us the secret of any victory, and if we don't lose the secret, we shall know final victory. It taught us that, contrary to what we sometimes used to think, the spirit is of no avail against the sword, but that the spirit together with the sword will always win out over the sword alone. That is why we have now accepted the sword, after making sure that the spirit was on our side. We had first to see people die and to run the risk of dying ourselves. We had to see a French workman walking toward the guillotine at dawn down the prison corridors and exhorting his comrades from cell to cell to show their courage. Finally, to possess ourselves of the spirit, we had to endure torture of our flesh. One really possesses only what one has paid for. We have paid dearly, and we have not finished paying. But we have our certainties, our justifications, our justice; your defeat is inevitable.

I have never believed in the power of truth in itself. But it is at least worth knowing that when expressed forcefully truth wins out over falsehood. This is the difficult equilibrium we have reached. This is the distinction that gives us strength as we fight today. And I am tempted to tell you that it so happens that we are fighting for fine distinctions, but the kind of distinctions that are as important as man himself. We are fighting for the distinction between sacrifice and mysticism, between energy and violence, between strength and cruelty, for that even finer distinction between the true and the false, between the man of the future and the cowardly gods you revere.

This is what I wanted to tell you, not above the fray but in the thick of the fray. This is what I wanted to answer to your remark, "You don't love your country," which is still haunting me. But I want to be clear with you. I believe that France lost her power and her sway for a long time to come and that for a long time she will need a desperate patience, a vigilant revolt to recover the element of prestige necessary for any culture. But I believe she has lost all that for reasons that are pure. And this is why I have not lost hope. This is the whole meaning of my letter. The man whom you pitied five years ago for being so reticent about his country is the same man who wants to say to you today, and to all those of our age in Europe and throughout the world: "I belong to an admirable and persevering nation which, admitting her errors and weaknesses, has not lost the idea that constitutes her whole greatness. Her people are always trying and her leaders are sometimes trying to express that idea even more clearly. I belong to a nation which for the past four years has begun to relive the course of her entire history and which is calmly and surely preparing out of the ruins to make another history and to take her chance in a game where she holds no trumps. This country is worthy of the difficult and demanding love that is mine. And I believe she is decidedly worth fighting for since she is worthy of a higher love. And I say that your nation, on the other hand, has received from its sons only the love it deserved, which was blind. A nation is not justified by such love. That will be your undoing. And you who were already conquered in your greatest victories, what will you be in the approaching defeat?"

July 1943

SECOND LETTER

I HAVE already written you once and I did so with a
tone of certainty. After five years of separation, I
told you why we were the stronger—because of the detour that took us out of our way to seek our justification,
because of the delay occasioned by worry about our
rights, because of the crazy insistence of ours on recon-
ciling everything that we loved. But it is worth repeating.
As I have already told you, we paid dearly for that detour. Rather than running the risk of injustice we preferred disorder. But at the same time that very detour
constitutes our strength today, and as a result we are
within sight of victory.

Yes, I have already told you all that and in a tone of
certainty, as fast as I could write and without erasing a
word. But I have had time to think about it. Night is a
time for meditation. For three years you have brought
night to our towns and to our hearts. For three years we
have been developing in the dark the thought which
now emerges fully armed to face you. Now I can speak
to you of the intelligence. For the certainty we now feel
is the certainty in which we see clearly and everything
stands out sharp and clear, in which the intelligence
gives its blessing to courage. And you who used to speak

flippantly of the intelligence are greatly surprised, I suppose, to see it return from the shadow of death and suddenly decide to play its role in history. This is where I
want to turn back toward you.

As I shall tell you later on, the mere fact that the heart
is certain does not make us any the more cheerful. This
alone gives a meaning to everything I am writing you.
But first I want to square everything again with you,
with your memory and our friendship. While I still can
do so, I want to do for our friendship the only thing one
can do for a friendship about to end—I want to make it
explicit. I have already answered the remark, "You don't
love your country," that you used to hurl at me and that
I still remember vividly. Today I merely want to answer your impatient smile whenever you heard the
word "intelligence." "In all her intelligences," you
told me, "France repudiates herself. Some of your intellectuals prefer despair to their country—others, the
pursuit of an improbable truth. We put Germany before
truth and beyond despair." Apparently that was true.
But, as I have already told you, if at times we seemed to
prefer justice to our country, this is because we simply
wanted to love our country in justice, as we wanted to
love her in truth and in hope.

This is what separated us from you; we made demands.
You were satisfied to serve the power of your nation and
we dreamed of giving ours her truth. It was enough for
you to serve the politics of reality whereas, in our wildest
aberrations, we still had a vague conception of the poli-

tics of honor, which we recognize today. When I say "we," I am not speaking of our rulers. But a ruler hardly matters.

At this point I see you smile as of old. You always distrusted words. So did I, but I used to distrust myself even more. You used to try to urge me along the path you yourself had taken, where intelligence is ashamed of intelligence. Even then I couldn't follow you. But today my answers would be more assured. What is truth, you used to ask? To be sure, but at least we know what falsehood is; that is just what you have taught us. What is spirit? We know its contrary, which is murder. What is man? There I stop you, for we know. Man is that force which ultimately cancels all tyrants and gods. He is the force of evidence. Human evidence is what we must preserve, and our certainty at present comes from the fact that its fate and our country's fate are linked together. If nothing had any meaning, you would be right. But there is something that still has a meaning.

It would be impossible for me to repeat to you too often that this is where we part company. We had formed an idea of our country that put her in her proper place, amid other great concepts—friendship, mankind, happiness, our desire for justice. This led us to be severe with her. But, in the long run, we were the ones who were right. We didn't bring her any slaves, and we debased nothing for her sake. We waited patiently until we saw clearly, and, in poverty and suffering, we had the joy of fighting at the same time for all we loved. You, on the other hand, are fighting against everything in man that does not belong to the mother country. Your sacrifices are inconsequential because your hierarchy is not the right one and because your values have no place. The heart is not all you betray. The intelligence takes its revenge. You have not paid the price it asks, not made the heavy contribution intelligence must pay to lucidity. From the depths of defeat, I can tell you that that is your downfall.

Let me tell you this story. Before dawn, from a prison I know, somewhere in France, a truck driven by armed soldiers is taking eleven Frenchmen to the cemetery where you are to shoot them. Out of the eleven, five or six have really done something: a tract, a few meetings, something that showed their refusal to submit. The five or six, sitting motionless inside the truck, are filled with fear, but, if I may say so, it is an ordinary fear, the kind that grips every man facing the unknown, a fear that is not incompatible with courage. The others have done nothing. This hour is harder for them because they are dying by mistake or as victims of a kind of indifference. Among them is a child of sixteen. You know the faces of our adolescents; I don't want to talk about them. The boy is dominated by fear; he gives in to it shamelessly. Don't smile scornfully; his teeth are chattering. But you have placed beside him a chaplain, whose task is to alleviate somewhat the agonizing hour of waiting. I believe I can say that for men who are about to be killed a conversation about a future life is of no avail. It is too hard to believe that the lime-pit is not the end of all. The prisoners in the truck are silent. The chaplain turns toward the child huddled in his corner. He will understand better. The child answers, clings to the chaplain's voice, and hope returns. In the mutest of horrors sometimes it is enough for a man to speak; perhaps he is going to fix everything. "I haven't done anything," says the child. "Yes," says the chaplain, "but that's not the question now. You must get ready to die properly." "It can't be possible that no one understands me." "I am your friend and perhaps I understand you. But it is late. I shall be with you and the Good Lord will be too. You'll see how easy it is." The child turns his head away. The chaplain speaks of God. Does the child believe in him? Yes, he believes. Hence he knows that nothing is as important as the peace awaiting him. But that very peace is what frightens the child. "I am your friend," the chaplain repeats.

The others are silent. He must think of *them*. The chaplain leans toward the silent group, turning his back on the child for a moment. The truck is advancing slowly with a sucking sound over the road, which is damp with dew. Imagine the gray hour, the early-morning smell of men, the invisible countryside suggested by sounds of teams being harnessed or the cry of a bird. The child leans against the canvas covering, which gives a little. He notices a narrow space between it and the truck body. He could jump if he wanted. The chaplain has his back turned and, up front, the soldiers are intent on finding their way in the dark. The boy doesn't stop to think; he tears the canvas loose, slips into the opening, and jumps. His fall is hardly heard, the sound of running on the road, then nothing more. He is in the fields, where his steps can't be heard. But the flapping of the

canvas, the sharp, damp morning air penetrating the
truck make the chaplain and the prisoners turn around.
For a second the priest stares at those men looking at him
in silence. A second in which the man of God must decide whether he is on the side of the executioners or on
the side of the martyrs in keeping with his vocation. But
he has already knocked on the partition separating him
from his comrades. *"Achtung!"* The alarm is given. Two
soldiers leap into the truck and point their guns at the
prisoners. Two others leap to the ground and start running across the fields. The chaplain, a few paces from the
truck, standing on the asphalt, tries to see them through
the fog. In the truck the men can only listen to the sounds
of the chase, the muffled exclamations, a shot, silence,
then the sound of voices again coming nearer, finally a
hollow stamping of feet. The child is brought back. He
wasn't hit, but he stopped surrounded in that enemy fog,
suddenly without courage, forsaken by himself. He is
carried rather than led by his guards. He has been
beaten somewhat, but not much. The most important
lies ahead. He doesn't look at the chaplain or anyone
else. The priest has climbed up beside the driver. An
armed soldier has taken his place in the truck. Thrown
into one of the corners, the child doesn't cry. Between the
canvas and the floor he watches the road slip away again
and sees in its surface a reflection of the dawn.

I am sure you can very well imagine the rest. But it is important for you to know who told me this story. It was a
French priest. He said to me: "I am ashamed for that
man, and I am pleased to think that no French priest

would have been willing to make his God abet murder." That was true. The chaplain simply felt as you do. It seemed natural to him to make even his faith serve his country. Even the gods are mobilized in your country. They are on your side, as you say, but only as a result of coercion. You no longer distinguish anything; you are nothing but a single impulse. And now you are fighting with the resources of blind anger, with your mind on weapons and feats of arms rather than on ideas, stubbornly confusing every issue and following your obsession. We, on the other hand, started from the intelligence and its hesitations. We were powerless against wrath. But now our detour is finished. It took only a dead child for us to add wrath to intelligence, and now we are two against one. I want to speak to you of wrath.

Remember, when I expressed amazement at the outburst of one of your superiors, you said to me: "That too is good. But you don't understand. There is a virtue the French lack—anger." No, that's not it, but the French are difficult on the subject of virtues. And they don't assume them unless they have to. This gives their wrath the silence and strength you are just beginning to feel. And it is with that sort of wrath, the only kind I recognize in myself, that I am going to end this letter.

For, as I told you, certainty is not gaiety of heart. We know what we lost on that long detour; we know the price we are paying for the bitter joy of fighting in agreement with ourselves. And because we have a keen sense of the irreparable, there is as much bitterness as confidence in our struggle. The war didn't satisfy us. We had not yet assembled our reasons for fighting. It is civil war, the obstinate, collective struggle, the unrecorded sacrifice that our people chose. This war is the one they chose for themselves instead of accepting it from idiotic or cowardly governments, a war in which they recognize themselves and are fighting for a certain idea they have formed of themselves. But this luxury they permitted themselves costs them a dreadful price. In this regard, too, my people deserve more credit than yours. For the best of their sons are the ones who are falling; that is my cruelest thought. In the derision of war there is the benefit of derision. Death strikes everywhere and at random. In the war we are fighting, courage steps up and volunteers, and every day you are shooting down our purest spirits. For your ingenuousness is not without foresight. You have never known what to select, but you know what to destroy. And we, who call ourselves defenders of the spirit, know nevertheless that the spirit can die when the force crushing it is great enough. But we have faith in another force. In raining bullets on those silent faces, already turned away from this world, you think you are disfiguring the face of our truth. But you are forgetting the obstinacy that makes France fight against time. That hopeless hope is what sustains us in difficult moments; our comrades will be more patient than the executioners and more numerous than the bullets. As you see, the French are capable of wrath.

December 1943

THIRD LETTER

UNTIL now I have been talking to you of my country and you must have thought in the beginning that my tone had changed. In reality, this was not so. It is merely that we didn't give the same meaning to the same words; we no longer speak the same language.

Words always take on the color of the deeds or the sacrifices they evoke. And in your country the word "fatherland" assumes blind and bloody overtones that make it forever alien to me, whereas we have put into the same word the flame of an intelligence that makes courage more difficult and gives man complete fulfillment. You have finally understood that my tone has really never changed. The one I used with you before 1939 is the one I am using today.

You will probably be more convinced by the confession I am going to make to you. During all the time when we were obstinately and silently serving our country, we never lost sight of an idea and a hope, forever present in us—the idea and the hope of Europe. To be sure, we haven't mentioned Europe for five years. But this is because you talked too much of it. And there too we were not speaking the same language; our Europe is not yours.

But before telling you what ours is, I want to insist that among the reasons we have for fighting you (they are the same we have for defeating you) there is perhaps none more fundamental than our awareness of having been, not only mutilated in our country, wounded in our very flesh, but also divested of our most beautiful images, for you gave the world a hateful and ridiculous version of them. The most painful thing to bear is seeing a mockery made of what one loves. And that idea of Europe that you took from the best among us and distorted has consequently become hard for us to keep alive in all its original force. Hence there is an adjective we have given up writing since you called the army of slavery "European," but this is only to preserve jealously the pure meaning it still has for us, which I want to tell you.

You speak of Europe, but the difference is that for you Europe is a property, whereas we feel that we belong to it. You never spoke this way until you lost Africa. That is not the right kind of love. This land on which so many centuries have left their mark is merely an obligatory retreat for you, whereas it has always been our dearest hope. Your too sudden passion is made up of spite and necessity. Such a feeling honors no one, and you can see why no European worthy of the name would accept it.

You say "Europe," but you think in terms of potential soldiers, granaries, industries brought to heel, intelligence under control. Am I going too far? But at least I know that when you say "Europe," even in your best moments, when you let yourselves be carried away by your own lies, you cannot keep yourselves from thinking of a cohort of docile nations led by a lordly

Germany toward a fabulous and bloody future. I should like you to be fully aware of this difference. For you Europe is an expanse encircled by seas and mountains, dotted with dams, gutted with mines, covered with harvests, where Germany is playing a game in which her own fate alone is at stake. But for us Europe is a home of the spirit where for the last twenty centuries the most amazing adventure of the human spirit has been going on. It is the privileged arena in which Western man's struggle against the world, against the gods, against himself is today reaching its climax. As you see, there is no common denominator.

Don't worry that I shall use against you the themes of an age-old propaganda; I shall not fall back on the Christian tradition. That is another problem. You have talked too much of it too, and, posing as defenders of Rome, you were not afraid to give Christ the kind of publicity he began to be accustomed to the day he received the kiss that marked him for torture. But, after all, the Christian tradition is only one of the traditions that made this Europe, and I am not qualified to defend it against you. To do so would require the instinct and inclination of a heart given over to God. You know this is not the case with me. But when I allow myself to think that my country speaks in the name of Europe and that when we defend one we are defending both, then I too have my tradition. It is the tradition both of a few great individuals and of an inexhaustible mass. My tradition has two aristocracies, that of the intelligence and that of courage; it has its intellectual leaders and its innumerable mass. Now tell me whether this Europe, whose frontiers are the genius of a few and the heart of all its inhabitants, differs from the colored spot you have annexed on temporary maps.

Remember, you said to me, one day when you were making fun of my outbursts: "Don Quixote is powerless if Faust feels like attacking him." I told you then that neither Faust nor Don Quixote was intended to attack the other and that art was not invented to bring evil into the world. You used to like exaggerated images and you continued your argument. According to you, there was a choice between Hamlet and Siegfried. At that time I didn't want to choose and, above all, it didn't seem to me that the West could exist except in the equilibrium between strength and knowledge. But you scorned knowledge and spoke only of strength. Today I know better what I mean and I know that even Faust will be of no use to you. For we have in fact accepted the idea that in certain cases choice is necessary. But our choice would be no more important than yours if we had not been aware that any choice was inhuman and that spiritual values could not be separated. Later on we shall be able to bring them together again, and this is something you have never been able to do. You see, it is still the same idea; we have seen death face to face. But we have paid dear enough for that idea to be justified in clinging to it. This urges me to say that your Europe is not the right one. There is nothing there to unite or inspire. Ours is a joint adventure that we shall continue to pursue, despite you, with the inspiration of intelligence.

I shan't go much further. Sometimes on a street corner,

in the brief intervals of the long struggle that involves us all, I happen to think of all those places in Europe I know well. It is a magnificent land molded by suffering and history. I relive those pilgrimages I once made with all the men of the West: the roses in the cloisters of Florence, the gilded bulbous domes of Krakow, the Hradschin and its dead palaces, the contorted statues of the Charles Bridge over the Ultava, the delicate gardens of Salzburg. All those flowers and stones, those hills and those landscapes where men's time and the world's time have mingled old trees and monuments! My memory has fused together such superimposed images to make a single face, which is the face of my true native land. And then I feel a pang when I think that, for years now, your shadow has been cast over that vital, tortured face. Yet some of those places are ones that you and I saw together. It never occurred to me then that someday we should have to liberate them from you. And even now, at certain moments of rage and despair, I am occasionally sorry that the roses continue to grow in the cloister of San Marco and the pigeons drop in clusters from the Cathedral of Salzburg, and the red geraniums grow tirelessly in the little cemeteries of Silesia.

But at other moments, and they are the only ones that count, I delight in this. For all those landscapes, those flowers and those plowed fields, the oldest of lands, show you every spring that there are things you cannot choke in blood. That is the image on which I can close. It would not be enough for me to think that all the great shades of the West and that thirty nations were on our side; I could not do without the soil. And so I know that everything in Europe, both landscape and spirit, calmly negates you without feeling any rash hatred, but with the calm strength of victory. The weapons the European spirit can use against you are the same as reside in this soil constantly reawakening in blossoms and harvests. The battle we are waging is sure of victory because it is as obstinate as spring.

And, finally, I know that all will not be over when you are crushed. Europe will still have to be established. It always has to be established. But at least it will still be Europe—in other words, what I have just written you. Nothing will be lost. Just imagine what we are now, sure of our reasons, in love with our country, carried along by all Europe, and neatly balanced between sacrifice and our longing for happiness, between the sword and the spirit. I tell you once more because I must tell you, I tell you because it is the truth and because it will show you the progress my country and I have made since the time of our friendship: henceforth we have a superiority that will destroy you.

April 1944

FOURTH LETTER

Man is mortal. That may be; but let us die resisting; and if our lot is complete annihilation, let us not behave in such a way that it seems justice!

OBERMANN, Letter 90

Now the moment of your defeat is approaching. I am writing you from a city known throughout the world which is now preparing against you a celebration of freedom. Our city knows this is not easy and that first it will have to live through an even darker night than the one that began, four years ago, with your coming. I am writing you from a city deprived of everything, devoid of light and devoid of heat, starved, and still not crushed. Soon something you can't even imagine will inflame the city. If we were lucky, you and I should then stand face to face. Then we could fight each other knowing what is at stake. I have a fair idea of your motivations and you can imagine mine.

These July nights are both light and heavy. Light along the Seine and in the trees, but heavy in the hearts of those who are awaiting the only dawn they now long for. I am waiting and I think of you; I still have one more thing to tell you—and it will be the last. I want to tell you how it is possible that, though so similar, we should be enemies today, how I might have stood beside you and why all is over between us now.

For a long time we both thought that this world had no ultimate meaning and that consequently we were cheated. I still think so in a way. But I came to different conclusions from the ones you used to talk about, which, for so many years now, you have been trying to introduce into history. I tell myself now that if I had really followed your reasoning, I ought to approve what you are doing. And this is so serious that I must stop and consider it, during this summer night so full of promises for us and of threats for you.

You never believed in the meaning of this world, and you therefore deduced the idea that everything was equivalent and that good and evil could be defined according to one's wishes. You supposed that in the absence of any human or divine code the only values were those of the animal world—in other words, violence and cunning. Hence you concluded that man was negligible and that his soul could be killed, that in the maddest of histories the only pursuit for the individual was the adventure of power and his only morality, the realism of conquests. And, to tell the truth, I, believing I thought as you did, saw no valid argument to answer you except a fierce love of justice which, after all, seemed to me as unreasonable as the most sudden passion.

Where lay the difference? Simply that you readily accepted despair and I never yielded to it. Simply that you saw the injustice of our condition to the point of being willing to add to it, whereas it seemed to me that man must exalt justice in order to fight against eternal injustice, create happiness in order to protest against the universe of unhappiness. Because you turned your despair into intoxication, because you freed yourself from it by making a principle of it, you were willing to destroy man's works and to fight him in order to add to his basic misery. Meanwhile, refusing to accept that despair and that tortured world, I merely wanted men to rediscover their solidarity in order to wage war against their revolting fate.

As you see, from the same principle we derived quite different codes, because along the way you gave up the lucid view and considered it more convenient (you would have said a matter of indifference) for another to do your thinking for you and for millions of Germans. Because you were tired of fighting heaven, you relaxed in that exhausting adventure in which you had to mutilate souls and destroy the world. In short, you chose injustice and sided with the gods. Your logic was merely apparent.

I, on the contrary, chose justice in order to remain faithful to the world. I continue to believe that this world has no ultimate meaning. But I know that something in it has a meaning and that is man, because he is the only creature to insist on having one. This world has at least the truth of man, and our task is to provide its justifications against fate itself. And it has no justification but man; hence he must be saved if we want to save the idea we have of life. With your scornful smile you will ask me: what do you mean by saving man? And with all my being I shout to you that I mean not mutilating him and yet giving a chance to the justice that man alone can conceive.

This is why we are fighting. This is why we first had to follow you on a path we didn't want and why at the end of that path we met defeat. For your despair constituted your strength. The moment despair is alone, pure, sure of itself, pitiless in its consequences, it has a merciless power. That is what crushed us while we were hesitating with our eyes still fixed on happy images. We thought that happiness was the greatest of conquests, a victory over the fate imposed upon us. Even in defeat this longing did not leave us.

But you did what was necessary, and we went down in history. And for five years it was no longer possible to enjoy the call of birds in the cool of the evening. We were forced to despair. We were cut off from the world because to each moment of the world clung a whole mass of mortal images. For five years the earth has not seen a single morning without death agonies, a single evening without prisons, a single noon without slaughters. Yes, we had to follow you. But our difficult achievement consisted in following you into war without forgetting happiness. And despite the clamors and the violence, we tried to preserve in our hearts the memory of a happy sea, of a remembered hill, the smile of a beloved face. For that matter, this was our best weapon, the one we shall never put away. For as soon as we lost it we should be as dead as you are. But we know now that the weapons of happiness cannot be forged without considerable time and too much blood.

We had to enter into your philosophy and be willing to resemble you somewhat. You chose a vague heroism, because it is the only value left in a world that has lost its meaning. And, having chosen it for yourselves, you chose it for everybody else and for us. We were forced to imitate you in order not to die. But we became aware then that our superiority over you consisted in our having a direction. Now that all that is about to end, we can tell you what we have learned—that heroism isn't much and that happiness is more difficult.

At present everything must be obvious to you; you know that we are enemies. You are the man of injustice, and there is nothing in the world that my heart loathes so much. But now I know the reasons for what was once merely a passion. I am fighting you because your logic is as criminal as your heart. And in the horror you have lavished upon us for four years, your reason plays as large a part as your instinct. This is why my condemnation will be sweeping; you are already dead as far as I am concerned. But at the very moment when I am judging your horrible behavior, I shall remember that you and we started out from the same solitude, that you and we, with all Europe, are caught in the same tragedy of the intelligence. And, despite yourselves, I shall still apply to you the name of man. In order to keep faith with ourselves, we are obliged to respect in you what you do not respect in others. For a long time that was your great advantage since you kill more easily than we do. And to the very end of time that will be the advantage of those who resemble you. But to the very end of time, we, who do not resemble you, shall have to bear witness so

that mankind, despite its worst errors, may have its justification and its proof of innocence.

This is why, at the end of this combat, from the heart
of this city that has come to resemble hell, despite all
the tortures inflicted on our people, despite our disfigured
dead and our villages peopled with orphans, I can tell
you that at the very moment when we are going to destroy
you without pity, we still feel no hatred for you. And
even if tomorrow, like so many others, we had to die, we
should still be without hatred. We cannot guarantee
that we shall not be afraid; we shall simply try to be
reasonable. But we can guarantee that we shall not hate
anything. And we have come to terms with the only
thing in the world I could loathe today, I assure you, and
we want to destroy you in your power without mutilating
you in your soul.

As for the advantage you had over us, you see that you
continue to have it. But it likewise constitutes our superiority. And it is what makes this night easy for me. Our
strength lies in thinking as you do about the essence of
the world, in rejecting no aspect of the drama that is ours.
But at the same time we have saved the idea of man at
the end of this disaster of the intelligence, and that idea
gives us the undying courage to believe in a rebirth. To
be sure, the accusation we make against the world is not
mitigated by this. We paid so dear for this new knowledge that our condition continues to seem desperate to
us. Hundreds of thousands of men assassinated at dawn,
the terrible walls of prisons, the soil of Europe reeking
with millions of corpses of its sons—it took all that to pay
for the acquisition of two or three slight distinctions

which may have no other value than to help some among us to die more nobly. Yes, that is heart-breaking. But we have to prove that we do not deserve so much injustice. This is the task we have set ourselves; it will begin tomorrow. In this night of Europe filled with the breath of summer, millions of men, armed or unarmed, are getting ready for the fight. The dawn about to break will mark your final defeat. I know that heaven, which was indifferent to your horrible victories, will be equally indifferent to your just defeat. Even now I expect nothing from heaven. But we shall at least have helped save man from the solitude to which you wanted to relegate him. Because you scorned such faith in mankind, you are the men who, by thousands, are going to die solitary. Now, I can say farewell to you.

July 1944

THE LIBERATION
OF PARIS

THE BLOOD OF FREEDOM

Paris is shooting all her bullets in the August night. In this vast setting of stones and waters, all around this river that has reflected so much history, the barricades of freedom have once more been thrown up. Once more justice must be bought with the blood of men.

We know this fight too well, we are too involved through our flesh and our hearts to accept this dreadful condition without bitterness. But we also know too well what is at stake to refuse the difficult fate that we must endure alone.

Time will bear witness to the fact that the men of France did not want to kill and that their hands were clean when they entered a war they had not chosen. Their reasons must then have been overwhelming for them suddenly to seize their guns and shoot steadily, in the night, at those soldiers who for two years thought the war was easy.

Yes, their reasons are overwhelming. They are as big as hope and as deep as revolt. They are the reasons of the future for a country that others tried so long to limit to the gloomy rumination of her past. Paris is fighting today so that France may speak up tomorrow. The people are under arms tonight because they hope for justice for tomorrow. Some go about saying that it is not worth while and that with a little patience Paris will be liberated without effort. But this is because they vaguely sense that this insurrection threatens many things that would continue to stand if all took place otherwise.

Indeed, this must be increasingly obvious: no one can think that a freedom torn from such convulsions will have the calm, tame aspect that some enjoy imagining. This dreadful travail will give birth to a revolution.

No one can hope that men who have fought in silence for four years and are now fighting all day long in the din of bombs and the crackle of guns will agree to the return of the forces of surrender and injustice under any circumstances. No one can expect that these men— the nation's best—will again accept doing what the best and purest did for twenty-five years—that is, loving their country in silence and silently despising her leaders. The Paris that is fighting tonight intends to command tomorrow. Not for power, but for justice; not for politics, but for ethics; not for the domination of France, but for her grandeur.

Our conviction is not that this will take place, but that this is taking place today in the suffering and obstinacy of the fight. And this is why, despite men's suffering, despite the blood and wrath, despite the dead who can never be replaced, the unjust wounds, and the wild bullets, we must utter, not words of regret, but words of hope, of the dreadful hope of men isolated with their fate.

This huge Paris, all black and warm in the summer night, with a storm of bombers overhead and a storm of snipers in the streets, seems to us more brightly lighted than the City of Light the whole world used to envy us. It is bursting with all the fires of hope and suffering, it has the flame of lucid courage and all the glow, not only of liberation, but of tomorrow's liberty.

COMBAT, *24 August 1944*

THE NIGHT OF TRUTH

WHILE the bullets of freedom are still whistling throughout the city, the cannons of the liberation are entering the gates of Paris amid shouts and flowers. In the most beautiful and hottest of August nights, the eternal stars over Paris mingle with the tracer bullets, the smoke of fires, and the colored rockets of a mass celebration. This unparalleled night marks the end of four years of monstrous history and of an unspeakable struggle in which France came to grips with her shame and her wrath.

Those who never despaired of themselves or of their country find their reward under this sky. This night is worth a world; it is the night of truth. Truth under arms and in the fray, truth sustained by force after having so long been empty-handed and unprotected. It is everywhere this night when people and cannons are booming simultaneously. It is the very voice of the people and the cannons; it wears the exhausted face of the street fighters, triumphal under their scars and sweat. Yes, it is indeed the night of truth, of the only truth that matters, the truth that is willing to fight and conquer.

Four years ago men rose up amid ruins and despair and calmly declared that nothing was lost. They said we had to carry on and that the forces of good could always

overcome the forces of evil if we were willing to pay the
price. They paid the price. And, to be sure, that price
was heavy; it had all the weight of blood and the dreadful
heaviness of prisons. Many of those men are dead,
whereas others have been living for years surrounded
by windowless walls. That was the price that had to be
paid. But those same men, if they could, would not
blame us for this terrible and marvelous joy that sweeps
us off our feet like a high tide.

For our joy has not broken faith with them. On the
contrary, it justifies them and declares that they were
right. United in the same suffering for four years, we
still are united in the same intoxication; we have won
our solidarity. And we are suddenly astonished to see
during this dazzling night that for four years we have
never been alone. We have lived the years of fraternity.

Harsh combats still await us. But peace will return to
this torn earth and to hearts tortured by hopes and
memories. One cannot always live on murders and
violence. Happiness and proper affection will have their
time. But that peace will not find us forgetful. And for
some among us, the faces of our brothers disfigured by
bullets, the great virile brotherhood of recent years will
never forsake us. May our dead comrades enjoy by themselves the peace that is promised us during this panting
night, for they have already won it. Our fight will be
theirs.

Nothing is given to men, and the little they can conquer is paid for with unjust deaths. But man's greatness
lies elsewhere. It lies in his decision to be stronger than
his condition. And if his condition is unjust, he has only

one way of overcoming it, which is to be just himself. Our truth of this evening, which hovers overhead in this August sky, is just what consoles man. And our hearts are at peace, just as the hearts of our dead comrades are at peace, because we can say as victory returns, without any spirit of revenge or of spite: "We did what was necessary."

COMBAT, 25 *August 1944*

THE FLESH

THE FLESH

IT WAS hard for us to speak of René Leynaud yesterday. Those who read in a corner of their newspaper that a Resistance journalist with that name had been shot by the Germans paid but fleeting attention to what for us was a dreadful, an atrocious announcement. And yet we must speak of him. We must speak of him so that the memory of the Resistance will be kept alive, not in a nation that may be forgetful, but at least in a few hearts that pay attention to human quality.

He had entered the Resistance during the first months. Everything that constituted his moral life, Christianity and respect for one's promise, had urged him to take his place silently in that battle of shadows. He had chosen the pseudonym that corresponded to everything purest in him; to all his comrades on *Combat* he was known as Clair.

The only private passion he had kept—along with that of personal modesty—was poetry. He had written poems that only two or three of us knew. They had the quality he himself had—transparency. But in the daily struggle he had given up writing, indulging only in buying the most varied books of poetry, which he was saving to read after the war. As for everything else, he shared our conviction that a certain language and insistence on

honesty would restore to our country the noble countenance we cherished. For months his place was waiting
for him on this newspaper, and with all the blindness of
friendship and affection we refused to accept the news of
his death. Today that is no longer possible.

He will no longer speak that language it was essential to speak. The absurd tragedy of the Resistance is
summed up in this frightful misfortune. For men like
Leynaud entered the struggle with the conviction that
no one had a right to speak until he had made a personal sacrifice. The trouble is that the unofficial war did
not have the dreadful justice of the regular war. At the
front, bullets strike at random, killing the best and the
worst. But for four years behind the lines, it was the best
who volunteered and fell, it was the best who earned the
right to speak, and lost the ability to do so.

In any case, the man we loved will never speak
again. And yet France needed voices like his. His ex-
ceptionally proud heart, protected by his faith and his
sense of honor, would have found the words we needed.
But he is now forever silent. And some who are not
worthy speak of the honor that was identified with him,
while others who are not trustworthy speak in the name
of the God he had chosen.

It is possible today to criticize the men of the Resistance, to note their shortcomings, and to bring accusations against them. But this is perhaps because the best
among them are dead. We say this because we are deeply
convinced of it: if we are still here, this is because we did
not do enough. Leynaud did enough. And today, having
been returned to the soil he enjoyed for so short a time,

having been cut off from that passion to which he had sacrificed everything, he may find consolation, we hope, in not hearing the words of bitterness and denigration now being applied to that poor human adventure in which we took part.

Never fear, we shall not make use of him, who never made use of anyone. He left the struggle unknown as he entered it unknown. We shall keep for him what he would have preferred—the silence of our hearts, an attentive memory, and the dreadful sorrow of the irreparable. But he will forgive us if we admit bitterness here where we have always tried to avoid it, and indulge in the thought that perhaps the death of such a man is too high a price to pay for granting others the right to forget in their behavior and their writings what was achieved during four years by the courage and sacrifice of a few Frenchmen.

COMBAT, *27 October 1944*

O<small>N THE</small> 16th of May 1944, René Leynaud, bearing secret documents, was arrested by members of the Vichy Militia in Place Bellecour at Lyon. When he tried to flee, a rain of bullets aimed at his legs stopped him. After a short stay in the hospital, he was transferred to Fort Montluc, where he was to remain incarcerated until the 13th of June 1944. That day the Germans who were getting ready to evacuate Lyon picked out nineteen prisoners at Montluc who were considered to have played an important part in the Resistance. We know the names of only eleven of them. Between five and six a.m., Leynaud and eighteen of his fellow prisoners were gathered together in the courtyard. They were served coffee and then handcuffed. One by one, they climbed into a truck, which took them to the Gestapo headquarters in Place Bellecour. They waited three quarters of an hour in the cellar of that building. When they were finally called, their handcuffs were removed and they were made to climb into the truck again with some German soldiers armed with machine guns. The truck drove out of Lyon in the direction of Villeneuve. At eleven o'clock it crept through Villeneuve and encountered a group of children returning from a walk. The prisoners and the children looked at each other for a time but

didn't exchange a word. Just beyond Villeneuve, opposite a grove of poplars, the truck stopped, the soldiers
leaped to the ground and commanded the men to get out
and go toward the woods. A first group of six left the
truck and started toward the trees. The machine guns
immediately crackled behind them and mowed them
down. A second group followed, then a third. Those
who were still breathing were put out of their pain by a
final shot. One of them, however, though frightfully
wounded, managed to drag himself to a peasant's house.
From him we learned the details. Leynaud's friends
simply wonder whether he was in the first group or one
of the later groups.

Leynaud was thirty-four. He was born on 24 August
1910 at Lyon-Vaise of parents from the Ardèche. He
had begun his education at the public school and gone
on to the Lycée Ampère in Lyon. While he was attend-
ing law school, he had begun as a journalist on *Le
Progrès* of Lyon. It was probably during the years just
before the war that he came to understand his love of
poetry and his profound Christianity.

In September 1939 Leynaud is mobilized, fights in
Lorraine, then in Belgium, takes part in the Dunkerque
retreat, and, being far away from the official evacuation,
nevertheless manages by some makeshift means to cross
the Channel to Plymouth. He returns to France and at
the moment of the armistice he is at Agen, sick and exhausted. I should like to point out, however, that none
of his friends ever heard Leynaud talk of the part he had
played in the war. We get these details from his wife.

Early in 1942 Leynaud made contact with Resistance
groups and was eventually to become local leader of
the *Combat* movement in Lyon under the pseudonym of
Clair.

For all of us, Leynaud's death made an example of
him. Yet before that we knew, just from the kind of at-
tachment we felt for him, that his life (and we have just
told the short, sharp story of that life) was exemplary.
Living very quietly, absorbed by the love of his wife and
his son, by the needs of the combat, he didn't have
many friends. But I have never known a single person
who, loving him, failed to love him without reservation.
This is because he inspired confidence. Insofar as it is
possible for a man, he gave himself completely to everything he did. He never bargained about anything, and
this is why he was assassinated. As solid as the short,
stocky oaks of his Ardèche, he was both physically and
morally strapping. Nothing could make the slightest
dent in him when he had once made up his mind what
was fair. It took a burst of bullets to subjugate him.

Up to now, I have spoken of Leynaud dryly and, so to
speak, in a general way. But if it is true that I shall
probably never again be able to speak freely of the man
who was my friend, at least I can try to set down now a
few more vivid images that I had already begun to put
together.

He was only slightly above average height, with thick,
curly hair, a rough-hewn face with gray eyes, a mobile
and rather full mouth, a broad nose, and a sharp jaw.

He dressed carelessly, but the shape of his body tended
to stretch his clothing and give it a certain elegance.

In 1943, on my way through Lyon, I often stayed in
his little room in Rue Vieille-Monnaie which his friends
knew so well. Leynaud would do the honors rapidly,
fussing about the bedside lamp and then, rising, would
take cigarettes out of an earthenware pot and share them
with me. "I smoke less than you," he would say, "and,
besides, I prefer my pipe." He would take it out, in fact,
and keep in in his mouth for a time. In my memory,
those hours have remained as classic examples of friendship. Leynaud, who was going to sleep somewhere else,
would stay until the curfew. All around us, the heavy
silence of the Occupation nights would settle down. That
big, somber city of conspiracy that Lyon then was would
gradually empty. But we would not speak of the conspiracy. As a matter of fact, Leynaud, unless he absolutely had to, never spoke of it. We would exchange
news of our friends. Sometimes we spoke of literature.
He loved the poets of the sixteenth century and especially the School of Lyon. His library, rare and precious,
which surrounded us then, was made up almost exclusively of poetry. But the poems came from all times and
all places. I did not have his competence. Yet I ventured
to tell him the impatience I felt when faced with the
short poem, the fleeting notation cultivated by so many
moderns. We saw eye to eye on that point, and it was
then that he told me of his plan for a long poem in which
he would try to set down what he had to say. Recovered
fragments of that poem figure in his volume of poetry.

But at that time Leynaud was not writing anything. He had decided that he would work *afterward*. From several indications, I guessed then that he was waiting impatiently for that *afterward*. This man who had never sidestepped any duty was to be especially congratulated because it so happened that he felt the full weight of duty. Fatigue would seize him at certain moments and give him that set look that would isolate him from the world for a time. He was too close to all he loved—his wife, his child, a certain way of life—not to dream of a future in which his love would not be endangered and in which he himself could be what he really was. "What will you do when it's all over?" he would ask me. But then as now I had no imagination and my replies were not clear. For Leynaud, everything was simple; he would resume his life at the point where he had left off, for he found it to his liking. Then, he had a child to raise. And though he rarely became animated, the name of his son was enough to make his eyes shine.

At other times we had less serious conversations. I used to like to see him laugh. He did so rarely, now that I stop to think about it, but then he would do so heartily, leaning back on his chair. The next moment he would be standing in a position in which I see him often, his feet apart, rolling his sleeves high above the elbows, and raising his vigorous arms to try to discipline his always tousled hair. We would talk of boxing, of swimming, and of camping. He loved the physical life, muscular effort, the fraternal earth, and all that in silence, just as he used to eat, with a lively, uncommunicative appetite. As midnight approached, he would empty his pipe, lay out more cigarettes that he urged me to smoke during the night, and, his coat over his arm, would set forth energetically. I could still hear him on the stairs as I looked around me at what belonged to him.

I also had meetings with him at Saint-Etienne. Between trains, we would spend a few hours in that hopeless town. I recall very vividly the first of those meetings, in September 1943, because everything about it was a disappointment. I had warned Leynaud that nothing could be accomplished at Saint-Etienne, where I used to stop off frequently then—that I was no good for anything in a city where I never felt anything but the most unreasonable torpor. In my opinion, if hell existed it would have to look like those interminable gray streets where everyone was wearing black. Leynaud assured me that I was exaggerating, and we made an appointment so that he could meet one of my friends whom he wanted to know. The friend was an energetic and irreverent Dominican who claimed to loathe the Christian Democrats and dreamed of a Nietzschean Christianity. Leynaud, who could not feel drawn to the cautious forms of Christianity, felt interested in that soldier-monk. Together with the priest, I was to wait for him at the Saint-Etienne station buffet. Unfortunately the priest, obliged to take a train early in the afternoon, had to lunch very early. Leynaud arrived finally during the dessert, but, suffering from a very obvious chest cold, he was hardly capable of talking coherently. Five minutes later my white-robed friend had to dash toward the platform. And Leynaud and I, whose trains did not leave until late in the afternoon, began to wander in hell, drugged

with heat and boredom, pausing at regular intervals in
front of a lemonade sweetened with saccharine in de-
serted cafés full of flies. Meanwhile he was stuffing himself with aspirin. Around four o'clock we were finally
able to talk a little. A bit later I took him to his train, and
he was already on the steps of the car when we both broke
out laughing. "You see," I said to him, "it's impossible to
accomplish anything here." He laughed heartily and, as
the train started up, he continued to laugh as he waved in
my direction. Of all the images I have of him, this one is
especially dear to me.

Another day, in Place Bellecour among playing children and the few pigeons that had escaped the inhabitants' hunger, Leynaud and I were talking of morality
and were of the opinion that, if I dare say so, something
should be done about it. That was the occasion when I
had a chance to measure what particularly distinguished
him, the force and quality of his silence, for we then
spent more than half an hour side by side apparently
absorbed in watching the passers-by but completely absorbed in pursuing a common thought.

The last time I saw him was in Paris in the spring of
1944. We were never closer to each other than during
that last meeting. We had met in a restaurant in Rue
Saint-Benoît, and afterward, walking along the quais in
beautiful weather, we had spoken at length of the future. We were in such deep agreement that for the first
time I felt an absolute confidence in the future of our
country. I cannot set down here our conversation although I have it all clearly in mind and several of his
letters still remind me that our words were as important

to him as they were to me. We had decided then to work together after the liberation. Leynaud was to settle in Paris and work for the same cause. But now he no longer belongs to anyone, and I shall take care not to give the impression that at present he would naturally be working with me. He left me that day at about four p.m. on the Pont du Carrousel. I am ashamed to say that I don't recall his last words. And I hadn't the slightest premonition as to his death. Sunk in stupid human confidence, sure of him and of his future, I merely waved at him from one end of the bridge to the other as he waved at me, with one arm in the air.

A few weeks before, he had written me: "May God grant us this year and a few others, and the joy of serving the same truth. These are my wishes for 1944 that I voice for you and for me because I am eager today not to dissociate you from a certain idea I have of myself, which is not, I hope, the least noble."

But that year was not granted him.

If I dared paraphrase one of his letters, I should say simply that I often consult in myself an image he put there, or a virtue, that bears his name and his countenance. Truth needs witnesses. Leynaud was one of them, and this is why I miss him today. With him here, I saw more clearly, and his death, far from making me better, as the books of consolation say, made my revolt more blind. The finest thing I can say in his favor is that he would not have followed me in that revolt. But no good is done to men by killing their friends, as I know only too well by now. And who can ever justify that dreadful death? What are duty, virtue, honors compared to what was irreplaceable in Leynaud? Yes, what are they but the paltry alibis of those who remain alive? We were cheated of a man three years ago, and since then we have had a heavy heart, that is all I can say. For us who loved him and for all those who, without knowing him, deserved to love him, this is a dead loss.

Introduction to Poésies posthumes, *by René Leynaud* (1947)

PESSIMISM
AND TYRANNY

PESSIMISM AND COURAGE

For some time now, articles have been appearing about works that are supposed to be pessimistic and consequently to lead directly to the most cowardly of all forms of subservience. The reasoning is elementary. A pessimistic philosophy is by its essence a philosophy of discouragement, and those who don't believe that the world is good are therefore said to be willing to serve tyranny. The most effective of those articles, because it was the best, was the one by M. George Adam in *Les Lettres Françaises*. M. Georges Rabeau in one of the recent issues of *L'Aube* makes the same accusation under the unacceptable title of "Nazism not dead?"

I see only one way of answering such a campaign, which is to answer openly. Although the problem goes beyond me, although it is aimed at Malraux, Sartre, and a few others more important than I, it would seem to me sheer hypocrisy not to speak in my own name. Yet I shall not insist on the basis of the argument. The idea that a pessimistic philosophy is necessarily one of discouragement is a puerile idea, but one that needs too long a refutation. I shall speak only of the method of thinking that inspired those articles.

Let me say at once that this method is reluctant to take facts into account. The writers who are the butt of the

articles have proved, as best as they could, that, though
they lacked philosophical optimism, man's duty, at least,
was not alien to them. Hence an objective mind would
be willing to say that a negative philosophy was not incompatible, in actual fact, with an ethics of freedom and
courage. Such a mind would see here merely an oppor-
tunity to learn something about the human heart.

That objective mind would be right. For the coexistence, in certain minds, of a philosophy of negation
and a positive morality illustrates, in fact, the great problem that is painfully disturbing the whole epoch. In a
word, it is a problem of civilization, and it is essential for
us to know whether man, without the help either of the
eternal or of rationalistic thought, can unaided create his
own values. Such an undertaking goes infinitely beyond
all of us. I say this because I believe it: France and Europe must now create a new civilization or else perish.

But civilizations are not built by rapping people on
the knuckles. They are built up by the confrontation of
ideas, by the blood of the spirit, by suffering and courage.
It is not possible that concepts which have belonged to
Europe for the past hundred years should be judged in
the twinkling of an eye, in *L'Aube*, by an editorialist
who, without hesitation, attributes to Nietzsche a lustful
appetite and to Heidegger the idea that existence is useless. I do not have much liking for the too famous existen-
tial philosophy, and, to tell the truth, I think its conclusions false. But at least it represents a great adventure
of the mind, and it is hard to see it subjected, by
M. Rabeau, to the judgment of the most shortsighted
conformism.

In reality, such concepts and such undertakings are not judged at this moment according to the rules of objectivity. They are judged not according to facts but according to a doctrine. Our Communist comrades and our Christian comrades talk to us from the vantage point of doctrines we respect. Their doctrines are not ours, but it has never occurred to us to talk of them in the tone they have just used toward us and with the assurance they show. Let us pursue then, insofar as we can, our experience and our thought. M. Rabeau blames us for having an audience. I believe that is an exaggeration. But this at least is true: the uneasiness that concerns us belongs to a whole epoch from which we do not want to dissociate ourselves. We want to think and live in our history. We believe that the truth of this age can be found only by living through the drama of it to the very end. If the epoch has suffered from nihilism, we cannot remain ignorant of nihilism and still achieve the moral code we need. No, everything is not summed up in negation and absurdity. We know this. But we must first posit negation and absurdity because they are what our generation has encountered and what we must take into account.

The men who are indicted in these articles are loyally attempting both in their work and in their lives to solve this problem. Is it so hard to realize that one cannot settle in a few lines a question others are not sure of solving when they devote themselves to it altogether? Can't they be granted the patience that is granted to any sincere undertaking? Isn't it possible to address them more humbly?

I shall end this protest here. I hope I have been restrained. But I should like my indignation to be felt. Objective criticism is the best of things, in my opinion, and I can't object when someone says that a work is bad or that a philosophy is not good for man's fate. It is only fair that writers should answer for their writings. That forces them to reflect, and we all have a dreadful need to reflect. But deriving from such principles judgments as to this or that mind's disposition toward slavery, especially when you have proof of the contrary, and concluding that this or that line of thought must necessarily lead to Nazism suggests an image of man which I prefer not to qualify and constitutes very paltry proof of the moral advantages of optimistic philosophy.

COMBAT, *September 1945*

DEFENSE OF INTELLIGENCE

(Speech given at the meeting organized by L'Amitié
Française on 15 March
1945)

I F THE kind of French friendship with which we are
concerned were to be but an effusion of feeling
among people who get along together, I should not count
on it. That would be the easiest, but also the least useful,
form of friendship. And I suppose that the people who
founded this society called L'Amitié Française wanted
something else—a more difficult form of friendship that
calls for effort. In order to avoid yielding to facility and
indulging in self-congratulation, I should like, in the
ten minutes allotted me, merely to point out the difficulties of such an undertaking. I could not possibly do
this more effectively than by speaking of what always
stands in the way of friendship—in other words, falsehood and hatred.

We shall indeed not accomplish anything for French
friendship if we cannot get rid of falsehood and hatred.
In a way, we have certainly not got rid of them. We
have been learning their lessons for too long now. And
perhaps the last and most long-lived victory of Hitlerism
is to be found in the shameful scars made on the hearts

of those who fought Hitlerism most vigorously. How
could it be otherwise? For years now, this world has been
subjected to an unparalleled outbreak of hatred. For four
years we witnessed here at home the reasoned expression
of that hatred. Men like you and me who in the morning
patted children on the head would a few hours later become meticulous executioners. Such men became the
bureaucrats of hatred and torture. For four years their
administration functioned by creating villages of orphans, by shooting men's faces full of holes so that they
would not be recognized, by jamming and stamping
children's bodies into coffins too small for them, by tor-
turing brothers in their sisters' presence, by shaping
cowards as in a mold, and by destroying the proudest of
souls. It seems that such stories are not believed abroad.
But for four years, in our anguish, we could not avoid believing them. Every morning for four years each Frenchman received his ration of hatred and his slap in the face
—when he opened his newspaper. Necessarily, some of
that has remained with us. We were left with hatred. We
were left with the impulse that the other day in Dijon
made a fourteen-year-old child fall upon a collaborator
who had been lynched and disfigure his face. We were
left with the rage that consumes our souls at the memory
of certain images and certain faces. The executioners'
hatred engendered the victims' hatred. And once the
executioners had gone, the French were left with their
hatred only partially spent. They still look at one another with a residue of anger.

Well, this is what we must overcome first of all. Our
poisoned hearts must be cured. And the most difficult

battle to be won against the enemy in the future must be fought within ourselves, with an exceptional effort that will transform our appetite for hatred into a desire for justice. Not giving in to hatred, not making any concessions to violence, not allowing our passions to become blind—these are the things we can still do for friendship and against Hitlerism. Even today certain newspapers still indulge in violence and insult. But that is simply still giving in to the enemy. Instead, it is essential that we never let criticism descend to insult; we must grant that our opponent may be right and that in any case his reasons, even though bad, may be disinterested. It is essential, in short, that we remake our political mentality.

What does this mean, if we stop to think about it? It means that we must save intelligence. A few years ago, when the Nazis had just seized power, Goering gave a fair idea of their philosophy by declaring: "When anyone talks to me of intelligence, I take out my revolver." And that philosophy was not limited to Germany. At the same time throughout civilized Europe the excesses of intelligence and the faults of the intellectual were being pointed out. Intellectuals themselves, by an interesting reaction, were not the last to join the attack. Everywhere philosophies of instinct were dominant and, along with them, the spurious romanticism that prefers feeling to understanding as if the two could be separated. Since then intelligence has regularly been blamed. The war came and then the defeat. Vichy taught us that the chief responsibility lay with the intelligence. Our peasants had read too much Proust. And everyone knows that

Paris-Soir, Fernandel, and trade-association banquets are signs of intelligence. It seems that the mediocrity of her leaders which was killing France had its source in books.

Even now intelligence is ill-treated. This proves simply that the enemy is not yet conquered. If you merely make an effort to understand without preconceptions, if you merely talk of objectivity, you will be accused of sophistry and criticized for having pretensions. No, we can't have that! That is what must be reformed. For I know as well as anyone the excesses of intelligence, and I know as well as anyone that the intellectual is a dangerous animal ever ready to betray. But that is not the right kind of intelligence. We are speaking of the kind that is backed by courage, the kind that for four years paid whatever was necessary to have the right to respect. When that intelligence is snuffed out, the black night of dictatorship begins. This is why we must maintain it with all its duties and all its rights. At that price, and only at that price, will French friendship have a meaning. For friendship is a knowledge acquired by free men. And there is no freedom without intelligence or without mutual understanding.

In conclusion, I shall speak directly to you students who are gathered here. I am not one to preach virtue to you. Too many Frenchmen confuse virtue with bloodlessness. If I had any right to do so, I should rather preach the passions to you. But I should like those who will represent French intelligence in the future to be resolved at least never to yield on one or two points. I should like them not to give in when they are told that intelligence is always unwelcome or that it is permissible to lie in order to succeed. I should like them not to give in to guile, to violence, or to inertia. Then perhaps a French friendship will be possible that will be more than idle talk. Then perhaps, in a nation that is free and passionately attached to truth, man will begin again to have that feeling for man, without which the world can never be but a vast solitude.

THE UNBELIEVER
AND CHRISTIANS

(Fragments of a statement made at the Dominican Monastery of Latour-Maubourg in 1948)

INASMUCH as you have been so kind as to invite a man who does not share your convictions to come and answer the very general question that you are raising in these conversations, before telling you what I think unbelievers expect of Christians, I should like first to acknowledge your intellectual generosity by stating a few principles.

First, there is a lay pharisaism in which I shall strive not to indulge. To me a lay pharisee is the person who pretends to believe that Christianity is an easy thing and asks of the Christian, on the basis of an external view of Christianity, more than he asks of himself. I believe indeed that the Christian has many obligations but that it is not up to the man who rejects them himself to recall their existence to anyone who has already accepted them. If there is anyone who can ask anything of the Christian, it is the Christian himself. The conclusion is that if I allowed myself at the end of this statement to demand of you certain duties, these could only be duties that it is essential to ask of any man today, whether he is or is not a Christian.

Secondly, I wish to declare also that, not feeling that I possess any absolute truth or any message, I shall never start from the supposition that Christian truth is illusory, but merely from the fact that I could not accept it. As an illustration of this position, I am willing to confess this: Three years ago a controversy made me argue against one among you, and not the least formidable. The fever of those years, the painful memory of two or three friends assassinated had given me the courage to do so. Yet I can assure you that, despite some excessive expressions on the part of François Mauriac, I have not ceased meditating on what he said. At the end of this reflection—and in this way I give you my opinion as to the usefulness of the dialogue between believer and unbeliever—I have come to admit to myself, and now to admit publicly here, that for the fundamentals and on the precise point of our controversy François Mauriac got the better of me.

Having said that, it will be easier for me to state my third and last principle. It is simple and obvious. I shall not try to change anything that I think or anything that you think (insofar as I can judge of it) in order to reach a reconciliation that would be agreeable to all. On the contrary, what I feel like telling you today is that the world needs real dialogue, that falsehood is just as much the opposite of dialogue as is silence, and that the only possible dialogue is the kind between people who remain what they are and speak their minds. This is tantamount to saying that the world of today needs Christians who remain Christians. The other day at the Sorbonne, speaking to a Marxist lecturer, a Catholic priest said in public that he too was anticlerical. Well, I don't like priests who are anticlerical any more than philosophies that are ashamed of themselves. Hence I shall not, as far as I am concerned, try to pass myself off as a Christian in your presence. I share with you the same revulsion from evil. But I do not share your hope, and I continue to struggle against this universe in which children suffer and die.

.   .   .   .

And why shouldn't I say here what I have written elsewhere? For a long time during those frightful years I waited for a great voice to speak up in Rome. I, an unbeliever? Precisely. For I knew that the spirit would be lost if it did not utter a cry of condemnation when faced with force. It seems that that voice did speak up. But I assure you that millions of men like me did not hear it and that at that time believers and unbelievers alike shared a solitude that continued to spread as the days went by and the executioners multiplied.

It has been explained to me since that the condemnation was indeed voiced. But that it was in the style of the encyclicals, which is not at all clear. The condemnation was voiced and it was not understood! Who could fail to feel where the true condemnation lies in this case and to see that this example by itself gives part of the reply, perhaps the whole reply, that you ask of me. What the world expects of Christians is that Christians should speak out, loud and clear, and that they should voice their condemnation in such a way that never a doubt, never the slightest doubt, could rise in the heart of the simplest man. That they should get away from abstraction and confront the blood-stained face history has taken on today. The grouping we need is a grouping of men resolved to speak out clearly and to pay up personally. When a Spanish bishop blesses political executions, he ceases to be a bishop or a Christian or even a man; he is a dog just like the one who, backed by an ideology, orders that execution without doing the dirty work himself. We are still waiting, and I am waiting, for a grouping of all those who refuse to be dogs and are resolved to pay the price that must be paid so that man can be something more than a dog.

.   .   .   .

And now, what can Christians do for us?

To begin with, give up the empty quarrels, the first of which is the quarrel about pessimism. I believe, for instance, that M. Gabriel Marcel would be well advised to leave alone certain forms of thought that fascinate him and lead him astray. M. Marcel cannot call himself a democrat and at the same time ask for a prohibition of Sartre's play. This is a position that is tiresome for everyone. What M. Marcel wants is to defend absolute values, such as modesty and man's divine truth, when the things that should be defended are the few provisional values that will allow M. Marcel to continue fighting someday, and comfortably, for those absolute values. . . .

By what right, moreover, could a Christian or a Marxist accuse me, for example, of pessimism? I was not the one to invent the misery of the human being or the terrifying formulas of divine malediction. I was not the one to shout *Nemo bonus* or the damnation of unbaptized children. I was not the one who said that man was incapable of saving himself by his own means and that in the depths of his degradation his only hope was in the grace of God. And as for the famous Marxist optimism! No one has carried distrust of man further, and ultimately the economic fatalities of this universe seem more terrible than divine whims.

Christians and Communists will tell me that their optimism is based on a longer range, that it is superior to all the rest, and that God or history, according to the individual, is the satisfying end-product of their dialectic. I can indulge in the same reasoning. If Christianity is pessimistic as to man, it is optimistic as to human destiny. Well, I can say that, pessimistic as to human destiny, I am optimistic as to man. And not in the name of a humanism that always seemed to me to fall short, but in the name of an ignorance that tries to negate nothing.

This means that the words "pessimism" and "optimism" need to be clearly defined and that, until we can do so, we must pay attention to what unites us rather than to what separates us.

. . . .

That, I believe, is all I had to say. We are faced with evil. And, as for me, I feel rather as Augustine did before becoming a Christian when he said: "I tried to find the source of evil and I got nowhere." But it is also true that I, and a few others, know what must be done, if not to reduce evil, at least not to add to it. Perhaps we cannot prevent this world from being a world in which children are tortured. But we can reduce the number of tortured children. And if you don't help us, who else in the world can help us do this?

Between the forces of terror and the forces of dialogue, a great unequal battle has begun. I have nothing but reasonable illusions as to the outcome of that battle. But

I believe it must be fought, and I know that certain men at least have resolved to do so. I merely fear that they will occasionally feel somewhat alone, that they are in fact alone, and that after an interval of two thousand years we may see the sacrifice of Socrates repeated several times. The program for the future is either a permanent dialogue or the solemn and significant putting to death of any who have experienced dialogue. After having contributed my reply, the question that I ask Christians is this: "Will Socrates still be alone and is there nothing in him and in your doctrine that urges you to join us?"

It may be, I am well aware, that Christianity will answer negatively. Oh, not by your mouths, I am convinced. But it may be, and this is even more probable, that Christianity will insist on maintaining a compromise or else on giving its condemnations the obscure form of the encyclical. Possibly it will insist on losing once and for all the virtue of revolt and indignation that belonged to it long ago. In that case Christians will live and Christianity will die. In that case the others will in fact pay for the sacrifice. In any case such a future is not within my province to decide, despite all the hope and anguish it awakens in me. I can speak only of what I know. And what I know—which sometimes creates a deep longing in me—is that if Christians made up their minds to it, millions of voices—millions, I say—throughout the world would be added to the appeal of a handful of isolated individuals who, without any sort of affiliation, today intercede almost everywhere and ceaselessly for children and for men.

WHY SPAIN?

(Reply to Gabriel Marcel)

I SHALL reply here to but two passages in your article on my *State of Siege* in the *Nouvelles Littéraires*. But I have no intention of replying to the criticisms that you or others made of the play as a dramatic work. When one indulges in publishing a book or staging a play, one has to accept the criticism it evokes. Whatever one may have to say, one must keep silent.

Yet you went beyond the critic's prerogatives when you expressed surprise that a play about totalitarian tyranny would be laid in Spain, whereas you would have been more inclined to imagine it in Eastern Europe. And when you state that the setting shows a lack of courage and fairness, you are asking for a reply. To be sure, you are kind enough to think that I am not responsible for the choice (this can be interpreted to mean that everything is the fault of Barrault, already so besmirched with crimes). Unfortunately, the play takes place in Spain because I alone chose, after much thought, that it should take place there. Consequently, I must take upon myself your accusations of opportunism and unfairness. And, under the circumstances, you will not be surprised that I feel obliged to answer you.

It is likely, moreover, that I should not defend myself against even these accusations (to whom can one justify oneself today?) if you had not touched on a sub-

ject as serious as that of Spain. For there is certainly no
need for me to say that I did not aim to flatter anyone by
writing *State of Siege*. I wanted to attack a kind of political society that set itself up, or is setting itself up, on a
totalitarian model, both on the Right and on the Left.
No one in good faith can fail to see that my play defends
the individual, the flesh in its noblest aspects—in short,
human love—against the abstractions and terrors of the
totalitarian state, whether Russian, German, or Spanish.
Every day pundits reflect about the decadence of our society and look for its basic causes. Most likely such causes
exist. But for the simpler among us the evil of our times
can be defined by its effects rather than by its causes.
That evil is the State, whether a police state or a
bureaucratic state. Its proliferation in all countries under
cover of the most varied ideological pretexts, the revolting security granted it by mechanical and psychological means of repression make of the State a mortal danger for everything that is best in each of us. From this
point of view, contemporary political society, in any form,
is despicable. This is just what I said, and this is why
State of Siege represents a break that aims to spare
nothing.

Once this has been stated clearly, why Spain? May I confess that I am somewhat ashamed to ask the question for
you? Why Guernica, Gabriel Marcel? Why that event
which for the first time, in the face of a world still sunk
in its comfort and its wretched morality, gave Hitler,
Mussolini, and Franco a chance to show even children
the meaning of totalitarian technique? Yes, why that

event, which concerned us too? For the first time men
of my age came face to face with injustice triumphing in
history. At that time the blood of innocence flowed amid
a chatter of pharisees, which, alas, is still going on. Why
Spain? Because there are some of us who will never wash
their hands of that blood. Anti-communism, whatever
reasons there may be for embracing it (and I know some
good ones), will never gain acceptance among us if it
forgets the injustice that is going on with the complicity
of our governments. I have stated as vigorously as I could
what I thought of the Russian concentration camps. But
they will not make me forget Dachau, Buchenwald, and
the nameless agony of millions, nor the dreadful repression that decimated the Spanish Republic. Yes, despite
the commiseration of our political leaders, all this together must be denounced at one and the same time.
And I cannot forgive that hideous plague in the West
of Europe because it is also ravaging the East on a
vaster scale. You write that, for the well-informed,
Spain is not now the source of the news most likely to
spread despair among men who respect human dignity.
You are not well informed, Gabriel Marcel. Just yesterday five political opponents were condemned to death
there. But you did everything you could to be ill informed by developing the art of forgetting. You have forgotten that the first weapons of totalitarian war were
bathed in Spanish blood. You have forgotten that in
1936 a rebellious general, in the name of Christ, raised
up an army of Moors, hurled them against the legally
constituted government of the Spanish Republic, won
victory for an unjust cause after massacres that can never

be expiated, and initiated a frightful repression that has lasted ten years and is not yet over. Yes, indeed, why Spain? Because you, like so many others, do not remember.

And also because, together with a small number of fellow Frenchmen, I am still occasionally not proud of my country. I do not know that France ever delivered up to the Russian government any anti-Stalinists who had taken refuge here. This will probably happen, for our leaders are ready for anything. In the case of Spain, however, the deed is already done. By virtue of the most disgraceful clause of the armistice, we handed over to Franco, on Hitler's orders, many Spanish republicans— among them the great Luis Companys. And Companys was shot while that frightful deal was going on. By Vichy, to be sure, and not by us. We merely put the poet Antonio Machado, back in 1938, into a concentration camp which he left only to die. But at that time when the French State rounded up victims for the totalitarian executioners, who voiced a protest? No one. That was probably, Gabriel Marcel, because those who might have protested shared your feeling that all that was a small matter compared to what they most loathed in the Russian system. So, after all, what did they care about one more man being shot by the firing squad? But the face of a man who has been shot by the firing squad is an ugly wound, and eventually gangrene sets in. The gangrene has spread.

Where then are the assassins of Companys? In Moscow or in our country? We must answer: in our country. We must admit that we shot Companys, that we are responsible for what followed. We must declare that we are ashamed, and that our only way of making up for this will be to preserve the memory of a Spain that was free and that we betrayed as best we could, in our own petty way. And it is true that no power failed to betray Spain, except Germany and Italy—and they shot Spaniards in open combat. But this can be no consolation, and free Spain continues, by its very silence, to ask amends of us. I did what I could, within the limits of my power, and this is what shocks you. If I had had more talent, the amends would have been greater; that is all I can say. But if I had compromised, that would have been cowardice and deceit. I shall not continue with this subject, however, and I shall stifle my feelings out of regard for you. At most let me add that no man of sensitivity should have been astonished that when I wanted to make a people of flesh and pride speak out against the shame and ghosts of dictatorship, I chose the Spanish people. I couldn't, after all, choose the international public of *Reader's Digest* or the readers of *Samedi-Soir* and *France-Dimanche*.

But you are doubtless eager for me to explain myself as to the role I gave the Church to play. On this point I shall be brief. You consider that role to be odious whereas it was not so in my novel.[1] But in my novel I had to do justice to those of my Christian friends whom I met during the Occupation in a combat that was just. In my play, on the other hand, I had to say what was the role of the Spanish Church. And if I made it odious, I did so because in the eyes of the world the role of the Spanish

[1] *The Plague.*

Church *was* odious. However unpleasant this truth may be for you, you can console yourself with the thought that the scene that bothers you lasts but a minute whereas the one that still offends the conscience of Europe has been going on for ten years. And the entire Church would have been sullied by the unbelievable scandal of Spanish bishops blessing the firing squad's rifles if during the very first days two great Christians— Bernanos, who is now dead, and José Bergamin, who is now exiled from his country—had not protested. Bernanos would not have written what you have written on this subject. *He* knew that the line with which my scene ends—"Spanish Christians, you have been abandoned" —does not insult your faith. *He* knew that if I had said something else or kept silent, I should then have insulted truth.

If I had to rewrite *State of Siege,* I should still set it in Spain; that is my conclusion. And, now and in the future, it would be obvious to everyone that the judgment pronounced in it transcends Spain and applies to all totalitarian societies. And no shameful complicity would have been involved. This is the way, and absolutely the only way, we can maintain the right to protest against a reign of terror. This is why I cannot share your opinion that we are in complete agreement in matters of politics. For you are willing to keep silent about one reign of terror in order the better to combat another one. There are some of us who do not want to keep silent about anything. It is our whole political society that nauseates us. Hence there will be no salvation until all those who are still worth while have repudiated it utterly in order to find, somewhere outside insoluble contradictions, the way to a complete renewal. In the meantime we must struggle. But with the knowledge that totalitarian tyranny is not based on the virtues of the totalitarians. It is based on the mistakes of the liberals. Talleyrand's remark is contemptible, for a mistake is not worse than a crime. But the mistake eventually justifies the crime and provides its alibi. Then the mistake drives its victims to despair, and that is why it must not be condoned. That is just what I cannot forgive contemporary political society: it is a mechanism for driving men to despair.

It will probably seem to you that I am getting very excited about a small matter. Then let me, for once, speak in my own name. The world I live in is loathsome to me, but I feel one with the men who suffer in it. There are ambitions that are not mine, and I should not feel at ease if I had to make my way by relying on the paltry privileges granted to those who adapt themselves to this world. But it seems to me that there is another ambition that ought to belong to all writers: to bear witness and shout aloud, every time it is possible, insofar as our talent allows, for those who are enslaved as we are. That is the very ambition you questioned in your article, and I shall consistently refuse you the right to question it so long as the murder of a man angers you only when that man shares your ideas.

COMBAT, *December 1948*

DEFENSE
OF FREEDOM

BREAD AND FREEDOM

(Speech given at the Labor
Exchange of Saint-Etienne
on 10 May 1953)

I F WE add up the examples of breach of faith and ex-
tortion that have just been pointed out to us, we
can foresee a time when, in a Europe of concentration
camps, the only people at liberty will be prison guards
who will then have to lock up one another. When only
one remains, he will be called the "supreme guard," and
that will be the ideal society in which problems of opposition, the headache of all twentieth-century governments, will be settled once and for all.

Of course, this is but a prophecy and, although governments and police forces throughout the world are
striving, with great good will, to achieve such a happy
situation, we have not yet gone that far. Among us, for
instance, in Western Europe, freedom is officially approved. But such freedom makes me think of the poor
female cousin in certain middle-class families. She has
become a widow; she has lost her natural protector.
So she has been taken in, given a room on the top floor,
and is welcome in the kitchen. She is occasionally
paraded publicly on Sunday, to prove that one is virtuous and not a dirty dog. But for everything else, and

especially on state occasions, she is requested to keep her mouth shut. And even if some policeman idly takes liberties with her in dark corners, one doesn't make a fuss about it, for she has seen such things before, especially with the master of the house, and, after all, it's not worth getting in bad with the legal authorities. In the East, it must be admitted, they are more forthright. They have settled the business of the female cousin once and for all by locking her up in a closet with two solid bolts on the door. It seems that she will be taken out fifty years from now, more or less, when the ideal society is definitively established. Then there will be celebrations in her honor. But, in my opinion, she may then be somewhat moth-eaten, and I am very much afraid that it may be impossible to make use of her. When we stop to think that these two conceptions of freedom, the one in the closet and the other in the kitchen, have decided to force themselves on each other and are obliged in all that hullabaloo to reduce still further the female cousin's activity, it will be readily seen that our history is rather one of slavery than of freedom and that the world we live in is the one that has just been described, which leaps out at us from the newspaper every morning to make of our days and our weeks a single day of revolt and disgust.

The simplest, and hence most tempting, thing is to blame governments or some obscure powers for such naughty behavior. Besides, it is indeed true that they are guilty and that their guilt is so solidly established that we have lost sight of its beginnings. But they are not the only ones responsible. After all, if freedom had always had to rely on governments to encourage her growth, she would probably be still in her infancy or else definitively buried with the inscription "another angel in heaven." The society of money and exploitation has never been charged, so far as I know, with assuring the triumph of freedom and justice. Police states have never been suspected of opening schools of law in the cellars where they interrogate their subjects. So, when they oppress and exploit, they are merely doing their job, and whoever blindly entrusts them with the care of freedom has no right to be surprised when she is immediately dishonored. If freedom is humiliated or in chains today, it is not because her enemies had recourse to treachery. It is simply because she has lost her natural protector. Yes, freedom is widowed, but it must be added because it is true: she is widowed of all of us.

Freedom is the concern of the oppressed, and her natural protectors have always come from among the oppressed. In feudal Europe the communes maintained the ferments of freedom; those who assured her fleeting triumph in 1789 were the inhabitants of towns and cities; and since the nineteenth century the workers' movements have assumed responsibility for the double honor of freedom and justice, without ever dreaming of saying that they were irreconcilable. Laborers, both manual and intellectual, are the ones who gave a body to freedom and helped her progress in the world until she has become the very basis of our thought, the air we cannot do without, that we breathe without even noticing it until the time comes when, deprived of it, we feel that we are dying. And if freedom is regressing today throughout such a large part of the world, this is prob-

ably because the devices for enslavement have never
been so cynically chosen or so effective, but also because
her real defenders, through fatigue, through despair, or
through a false idea of strategy and efficiency, have
turned away from her. Yes, the great event of the
twentieth century was the forsaking of the values of
freedom by the revolutionary movement, the progressive
retreat of socialism based on freedom before the attacks
of a Caesarian and military socialism. Since that moment
a certain hope has disappeared from the world and a solitude has begun for each and every free man.

When, after Marx, the rumor began to spread and
gain strength that freedom was a bourgeois hoax, a single word was misplaced in that definition, and we are still
paying for that mistake through the convulsions of our
time. For it should have been said merely that bourgeois
freedom was a hoax—and not all freedom. It should
have been said simply that bourgeois freedom was not
freedom or, in the best of cases, was not yet freedom.
But that there were liberties to be won and never to be
relinquished again. It is quite true that there is no possible freedom for the man tied to his lathe all day long who,
when evening comes, crowds into a single room with
his family. But this fact condemns a class, a society and
the slavery it assumes, not freedom itself, without
which the poorest among us cannot get along. For even if
society were suddenly transformed and became decent
and comfortable for all, it would still be a barbarous state
unless freedom triumphed. And because bourgeois society talks about freedom without practicing it, must the
world of workers also give up practicing it and boast

merely of not talking about it? Yet the confusion took place and in the revolutionary movement freedom was gradually condemned because bourgeois society used it as a hoax. From a justifiable and healthy distrust of the way that bourgeois society prostituted freedom, people came to distrust freedom itself. At best, it was postponed to the end of time, with the request that meanwhile it be not talked about. The contention was that we needed justice first and that we would come to freedom later on, as if slaves could ever hope to achieve justice. And forceful intellectuals announced to the worker that bread alone interested him rather than freedom, as if the worker didn't know that his bread depends in part on his freedom. And, to be sure, in the face of the prolonged injustice of bourgeois society, the temptation to go to such extremes was great. After all, there is probably not one of us here who, either in deed or in thought, did not succumb. But history has progressed, and what we have seen must now make us think things over. The revolution brought about by workers succeeded in 1917 and marked the dawn of real freedom and the greatest hope the world has known. But that revolution, surrounded from the outside, threatened within and without, provided itself with a police force. Inheriting a definition and a doctrine that pictured freedom as suspect, the revolution little by little became stronger, and the world's greatest hope hardened into the world's most efficient dictatorship. The false freedom of bourgeois society has not suffered meanwhile. What was killed in the Moscow trials and elsewhere, and in the revolutionary camps, what is assassinated when in Hungary a railway worker is shot for some professional mistake, is not bourgeois freedom but rather the freedom of 1917. Bourgeois freedom can meanwhile have recourse to all possible hoaxes. The trials and perversions of revolutionary society furnish it at one and the same time with a good conscience and with arguments against its enemies.

In conclusion, the characteristic of the world we live in is just that cynical dialectic which sets up injustice against enslavement while strengthening one by the other. When we admit to the palace of culture Franco, the friend of Goebbels and of Himmler—Franco, the real victor of the Second World War—to those who protest that the rights of man inscribed in the charter of UNESCO are turned to ridicule every day in Franco's prisons we reply without smiling that Poland figures in UNESCO too and that, as far as public freedom is concerned, one is no better than the other. An idiotic argument, of course! If you were so unfortunate as to marry off your elder daughter to a sergeant in a battalion of ex-convicts, this is no reason why you should marry off her younger sister to the most elegant detective on the society squad; one black sheep in the family is enough. And yet the idiotic argument works, as is proved to us every day. When anyone brings up the slave in the colonies and calls for justice, he is reminded of prisoners in Russian concentration camps, and vice versa. And if you protest against the assassination in Prague of an opposition historian like Kalandra, two or three American Negroes are thrown in your face. In such a disgusting attempt at outbidding, one thing only does not change—the victim, who is always the same. A single value is constantly outraged or prostituted—freedom—and then we notice that everywhere, together with freedom, justice is also profaned.

How then can this infernal circle be broken? Obviously, it can be done only by reviving at once, in ourselves and in others, the value of freedom—and by never again agreeing to its being sacrificed, even temporarily, or separated from our demand for justice. The current motto for all of us can only be this: without giving up anything on the plane of justice, yield nothing on the plane of freedom. In particular, the few democratic liberties we still enjoy are not unimportant illusions that we can allow to be taken from us without a protest. They represent exactly what remains to us of the great revolutionary conquests of the last two centuries. Hence they are not, as so many clever demagogues tell us, the negation of true freedom. There is no ideal freedom that will someday be given us all at once, as a pension comes at the end of one's life. There are liberties to be won painfully, one by one, and those we still have are stages—most certainly inadequate, but stages nevertheless—on the way to total liberation. If we agree to suppress them, we do not progress nonetheless. On the contrary, we retreat, we go backward, and someday we shall have to retrace our steps along that road, but that new effort will once more be made in the sweat and blood of men.

No, choosing freedom today does not mean ceasing to be a profiteer of the Soviet regime and becoming a profiteer of the bourgeois regime. For that would amount, instead, to choosing slavery twice and, as a final condemnation, choosing it twice for others. Choosing freedom is not, as we are told, choosing against justice. On the other hand, freedom is chosen today in relation to those who are everywhere suffering and fighting, and this is the only freedom that counts. It is chosen at the same time as justice, and, to tell the truth, henceforth we cannot choose one without the other. If someone takes away your bread, he suppresses your freedom at the same time. But if someone takes away your freedom, you may be sure that your bread is threatened, for it depends no longer on you and your struggle but on the whim of a master. Poverty increases insofar as freedom retreats throughout the world, and vice versa. And if this cruel century has taught us anything at all, it has taught that the economic revolution must be free just as liberation must include the economic. The oppressed want to be liberated not only from their hunger but also from their masters. They are well aware that they will be effectively freed of hunger only when they hold their masters, all their masters, at bay.

I shall add in conclusion that separating freedom from justice is tantamount to separating culture and labor, which is the epitome of the social sin. The confusion of the workers' movement in Europe springs in part from the fact that it has lost its real home, where it took comfort after all defeats, which was its faith in freedom. But, likewise, the confusion of European intellectuals springs from the fact that the double hoax, bourgeois and pseudo-revolutionary, separated them from their sole source of authenticity, the work and suffering of all, cutting them off from their sole natural allies, the workers. Insofar as I am concerned, I have recognized only two aristocracies, that of labor and that of the intelligence, and I know now that it is mad and criminal to try to make one dominate the other. I know that the two of them constitute but a single nobility, that their truth and, above all, their effectiveness lie in union; I know that if they are separated, they will allow themselves to be overcome gradually by the forces of tyranny and barbarousness, but that united, on the other hand, they will govern the world. This is why any undertaking that aims to loosen their ties and separate them is directed against man and his loftiest hopes. The first concern of any dictatorship is, consequently, to subjugate both labor and culture. In fact, both must be gagged or else, as tyrants are well aware, sooner or later one will speak up for the other. Thus, in my opinion, there are two ways for an intellectual to betray at present, and in both cases he betrays because he accepts a single thing—that separation between labor and culture. The first way is characteristic of bourgeois intellectuals who are willing that their privileges should be paid for by the enslavement of the workers. They often say that they are defending freedom, but they are defending first of all the privileges freedom gives to them, and to them alone.[1] The second way is characteristic of intellectuals who think they are leftist and who, through distrust of freedom, are willing that culture, and the freedom it presupposes, should be directed, under the vain pretext of serving a future justice. In both cases the profiteers of injustice and the renegades of freedom ratify and sanction the separation

[1] And, besides, most of the time they do not even defend freedom the moment there is any risk in doing so.

of intellectual and manual labor which condemns both labor and culture to impotence. They depreciate at one and the same time both freedom and justice.

It is true that freedom, when it is made up principally of privileges, insults labor and separates it from culture. But freedom is not made up principally of privileges; it is made up especially of duties. And the moment each of us tries to give freedom's duties precedence over its privileges, freedom joins together labor and culture and sets in motion the only force that can effectively serve justice. The rule of our action, the secret of our resistance can be easily stated: everything that humiliates labor also humiliates the intelligence, and vice versa. And the revolutionary struggle, the centuries-old straining toward liberation can be defined first of all as a double and constant rejection of humiliation.

To tell the truth, we have not yet cast off that humiliation. But the wheel turns, history changes, and a time is coming, I am sure, when we shall cease to be alone. For me, our gathering here today is in itself a sign. The fact that members of unions gather together and crowd around our freedoms to defend them is indeed reason enough for all to come here from all directions to illustrate their union and their hope. The way ahead of us is long. Yet if war does not come and mingle everything in its hideous confusion, we shall have time at last to give a form to the justice and freedom we need. But to achieve that we must henceforth categorically refuse, without anger but irrevocably, the lies with which we have been stuffed. No, freedom is not founded on concentration camps, or on the subjugated peoples of the colonies, or on the workers' poverty! No, the doves of peace do not perch on gallows! No, the forces of freedom cannot mingle the sons of the victims with the executioners of Madrid and elsewhere! Of that, at least, we shall henceforth be sure, as we shall be sure that freedom is not a gift received from a State or a leader but a possession to be won every day by the effort of each and the union of all.

98

HOMAGE TO AN EXILE

(Speech delivered 7 December 1955 at a banquet in honor of President Eduardo Santos, editor of *El Tiempo*, driven out of Colombia by the dictatorship)

PROUDLY we receive among us this evening an ambassador who is not like other ambassadors. Indeed, I have read that the government that had the sorry privilege of suppressing the greatest newspaper in South America had previously offered its editor, President Eduardo Santos, an ambassadorship to Paris. You refused that honor, Mr. President, not out of scorn for Paris, we are well aware, but out of love for Colombia, and probably because you know that governments often look upon foreign embassies as places of gilded expatriation for citizens who are in the way. You remained in Bogotá, as your conscience dictated; hence you were in the way, and you were censored without diplomatic respect and in the most cynical fashion possible. But at the same time you were provided with all the titles that justify your being considered today by all of us as the true ambassador of Colombia, not only in Paris but in every capital where the single word "liberty" makes hearts beat faster.

It is not so easy as people think to be a free man. In

truth, the only ones who assert that it is easy are those who have decided to forego freedom. For freedom is refused not because of its privileges, as some would have us believe, but because of its exhausting tasks. For those, on the other hand, whose function and passion consist in granting liberty all its rights and duties, know that this requires a daily effort and a constant vigilance in which pride and humility play equal parts. If we are tempted today, Mr. President, to express all our affection for you—at the same time as to Mr. Roberto García Peñas—this is because you maintained that constant vigilance without ever sparing yourself. By refusing the dishonor that was offered you (which amounted to taking upon yourself the repudiation and penance a government dared to impose on you), by letting your fine newspaper be destroyed rather than allowing it to serve falsehood and despotism, you were one of those uncompromising witnesses who, in all circumstances, deserve respect. But that would not yet suffice to make of you a witness of liberty. Many men have sacrificed everything to errors, and I have always thought that heroism and sacrifice were not enough to justify a cause. Obstinacy alone is not a virtue. What, on the other hand, gives your resistance its true meaning, what makes of you the exemplary companion we are eager to greet, is that under the same circumstances—when you were the respected President of Colombia—you not only did not use your power to censor your adversaries but you kept the newspaper of your political enemies from being suppressed.

That deed alone is enough for us to recognize in you a

real free man. Liberty has sons who are not all legitimate
or to be admired. Those who applaud it only when it
justifies their privileges and shout nothing but censorship when it threatens them are not on our side. But
those who, according to Benjamin Constant's remark,
are willing neither to suffer nor to possess the means of
oppression, who want freedom both for themselves and
for others—they, in an age that poverty or terror condemns to the excesses of oppression, are the seeds be-
neath the snow of which one of the greatest among us
spoke. Once the storm is over, the world will live off
them.

Such men, we know, are rare. Today freedom has not
many allies. I have been known to say that the real passion of the twentieth century was slavery. That was a
bitter remark which did an injustice to all those men
(you are one of them) whose sacrifice and example every
day help us to live. But I merely wanted to express that
anguish I feel every day when faced with the decrease
of liberal energies, the prostituting of words, the
slandered victims, the smug justification of oppression,
the insane admiration of force. We see a multiplication
of those minds of whom it has been said that they seemed
to count an inclination toward slavery as an ingredient of
virtue. We see the intelligence seeking justifications
for its fear, and finding them readily, for every cowardice
has its own philosophy. Indignation is measured,
silences take counsel from one another, and history has
ceased to be anything but Noah's cloak that is spread
over the victims' obscenity. In short, all flee real responsibility, the effort of being consistent or of having an

opinion of one's own, in order to take refuge in the parties or groups that will think for them, express their anger for them, and make their plans for them. Contemporary intelligence seems to measure the truth of doctrines and causes solely by the number of armored divisions that each can put into the field. Thenceforth everything is good that justifies the slaughter of freedom, whether it be the nation, the people, or the grandeur of the State. The welfare of the people in particular has always been the alibi of tyrants, and it provides the further advantage of giving the servants of tyranny a good conscience. It would be easy, however, to destroy that good conscience by shouting to them: if you want the happiness of the people, let them speak out and tell what kind of happiness they want and what kind they don't want! But, in truth, the very ones who make use of such alibis know they are lies; they leave to their intellectuals on duty the chore of believing in them and of proving that religion, patriotism, and justice need for their survival the sacrifice of freedom. As if freedom, when it leaves a certain place, were not the last to go, after all that constituted our reasons for living. No, freedom does not die alone. At the same time justice is forever exiled, the nation begins to agonize, and innocence is crucified anew every day.

To be sure, freedom is not the answer to everything, and it has frontiers. The freedom of each finds its limits in that of others; no one has a right to absolute freedom. The limit where freedom begins and ends, where its rights and duties come together, is called law, and the State itself must bow to the law. If it evades the

law, if it deprives the citizens of the benefits of the
law, there is breach of faith. Last August there was
breach of faith in Colombia, just as there has been
breach of faith in Spain for the last twenty years. And
there again your example helps to remind us that there is
no compromise with breach of faith. One has to reject
it and fight it.

Your battlefield was the press. Freedom of the press is
perhaps the freedom that has suffered the most from the
gradual degradation of the idea of liberty. The press has
its pimps as it has its policemen. The pimp debases it,
the policeman subjugates it, and each uses the other as a
way of justifying his own abuses. Those gentlemen vie
with each other in protecting the orphan and giving her
shelter, whether that shelter is a prison or a house of
prostitution. The orphan, indeed, is justified in de-
clining such eager offers of help and in deciding that she
must fight alone and alone resolve her fate.

Not that the press in itself is an absolute good. Victor
Hugo said in a speech that it was intelligence, progress,
and I know not what else. The already-old journalist I
am knows that it is nothing of the sort and that reality is
less consoling. But in another sense the press is better
than intelligence or progress; it is the possibility of all
that and of other things as well. A free press can of course
be good or bad, but, most certainly, without freedom it
will never be anything but bad. When one knows of
what man is capable, for better and for worse, one also
knows that it is not the human being himself who must
be protected but the possibilities he has within him—in
other words, his freedom. I confess, insofar as I am con-

cerned, that I cannot love all humanity except with a vast
and somewhat abstract love. But I love a few men, living
or dead, with such force and admiration that I am always
eager to preserve in others what will someday perhaps
make them resemble those I love. Freedom is nothing
else but a chance to be better, whereas enslavement is a
certainty of the worst.

If then, despite so many compromises or servilities, we
are to continue seeing journalism, when it is free, as one
of the greatest professions of the time, this is only because it allows men like you and your collaborators to
serve their country and their time on the highest level.
With freedom of the press, nations are not sure of going
toward justice and peace. But without it, they are sure of
not going there. For justice is done to peoples only when
their rights are recognized, and there is no right without
expression of that right. On this point we can take the
word of Rosa Luxembourg, who said: "Without unlim-
ited freedom of the press, without absolute freedom of
association, the dominant power of large popular masses
is inconceivable."

Consequently, we must be adamant as to the principle
of that freedom. It is not merely the basis of cultural
privileges, as people try hypocritically to convince us. It
is also the basis for the rights of labor. Those who, the
better to justify their tyrannies, set in opposition labor
and culture will not make us forget that whatever subjects the intelligence enchains labor, and vice versa.
When intelligence is gagged, the worker is soon subjugated, just as when the proletariat is enslaved the intellectual is soon reduced to silence or to lies. In short,

whoever does violence to truth or to its expression eventually mutilates justice, even though he thinks he is serving it. From this point of view, we shall deny to the very end that a press is true because it is revolutionary; it will be revolutionary only if it is true, and never otherwise. So long as we keep in mind these facts, your resistance, Mr. President, will preserve its real meaning, and, far from being a solitary example, it will throw light on the long struggle that you will be helping us not to abandon.

The Colombian government accused *El Tiempo* of being a super-State within the State, and you were right to refute that argument. But your government was right too, although in a way that it could not accept. For, by saying that, it paid homage to the power of the printed word. Censorship and oppression prove that the word is enough to make the tyrant tremble—but only if the word is backed up by sacrifice. For only the word fed by blood and heart can unite men, whereas the silence of tyrannies separates them. Tyrants indulge in monologues over millions of solitudes. If we reject oppression and falsehood, on the other hand, this is because we reject solitude. Every insubordinate person, when he rises up against oppression, reaffirms thereby the solidarity of all men. No, it is not you or a distant newspaper that you defended by resisting oppression, but the entire community that unites us over and above frontiers.

Is it not true, moreover, that throughout the world your name has always been linked to the cause of freedom? How can we fail to recall here that you were and still are one of the most faithful friends of our Spain, of

Republican Spain, today scattered throughout the world, betrayed by its allies and its friends, forgotten by all, humiliated Spain which stands erect solely by the force of its protest? The day when the other Spain, the Spain of churches and prisons, enters with its jailers and its censors into the organization of so-called free nations, I know that on that day you will stand with all of us, silently but with no spirit of revenge, beside free and suffering Spain.

For such fidelity let me thank you in the name of my second country and in the name of all those who, gathered here, bespeak their gratitude and their friendship. We thank you for being among those few who, in a time of enslavement and fear, stand firm on their right. People are complaining almost everywhere that the sense of duty is disappearing. How could it be otherwise since no one cares any more about his rights? Only he who is uncompromising as to his rights maintains the sense of duty. The great citizens of a country are not those who bend the knee before authority but rather those who, against authority if need be, are adamant as to the honor and freedom of that country. And your country will always recognize in you its great citizen, as we are doing here, because you, scorning all opportunism, managed to bear up against the total injustice that was inflicted upon you. At a moment when the most shortsighted realism, a debased conception of power, the passion for dishonor, and the ravages of fear disfigure the world, at the very moment when it is possible to think that all is lost, something on the other hand is beginning, since we have nothing more to lose. What is beginning is the period of the indomitable men devoted to the unconditional defense of liberty. This is why your attitude serves as an example and a comfort to all those who, like me, have now broken with many of their traditional friends by rejecting any complicity, even temporary, even and above all tactical, with regimes or parties whether of the Right or of the Left that justify, however little, the suppression of a single one of our liberties!

In conclusion, allow me to say that, reading the other day the wonderful message you addressed to your people, I appreciated not only your steadfastness and constancy but also the long suffering you must have experienced. When oppression wins out, as we all know here, those who nevertheless believe that their cause is just suffer from a sort of astonishment upon discovering the apparent impotence of justice. Then come the hours of exile and solitude that we have all known. Yet I should like to tell you that, in my opinion, the worst thing that can happen in the world we live in is for one of those men of freedom and courage I have described to stagger under the weight of isolation and prolonged adversity, to doubt himself and what he represents. And it seems to me that at such a moment those who are like him must come toward him (forgetting his titles and all devices of the official orator) to tell him straight from the heart that he is not alone and that his action is not futile, that there always comes a day when the palaces of oppression crumble, when exile comes to an end, when liberty catches fire. Such calm hope justifies your action. If, after all, men cannot always make history have a meaning, they can always act so that their own lives have one. Believe me when I tell you that across thousands of miles, all the way from far-off Colombia, you and your collaborators have shown us a part of the difficult road we must travel together toward liberty. And allow me, in the name of the faithful and grateful friends receiving you here, to greet fraternally in you and your collaborators the great companions of our common liberation.

ALGERIA

PREFACE TO ALGERIAN REPORTS

HERE is a group of selected articles and texts concerning Algeria. They are spaced out over a period of twenty years—from 1939, when almost no one in France was interested in that country, until 1958, when everyone talks about it. A volume would not have been enough to contain all the articles. It was necessary to eliminate the repetitions and too general commentaries and preserve the facts, figures, and suggestions that may still be useful. As they stand, these texts sum up the position of a man who, faced very young with the misery of Algeria, in vain multiplied his warnings and, long aware of his country's responsibilities, cannot approve a policy of preservation or oppression in Algeria. But I have long been alert to Algerian realities and cannot approve, either, a policy of surrender that would abandon the Arab people to an even greater misery, tear the French in Algeria from their century-old roots, and favor, to no one's advantage, the new imperialism now threatening the liberty of France and of the West.

Such a position satisfies no one today, and I know in advance how it will be received by both sides. I sincerely regret it, but I cannot do violence to what I feel and what I believe. Besides, on this subject no one satisfies me either. This is why, finding it impossible to join ei-

ther extreme camp, faced with the gradual disappearance
of that third camp in which it was still possible to keep a
cool head, doubting my certainties and the things I
thought I knew, convinced in short that the real cause of
our follies is to be found in the habits and functioning of
our intellectual and political society, I decided to take no
further part in the constant polemics that have had no result other than to harden the uncompromising points of
view at loggerheads in Algeria and to split even wider a
France already poisoned by hatreds and sects.

There is indeed a spitefulness in the French, and I
refuse to add to it. I know only too well what it has cost
us and still costs us. For the past twenty years the French
have loathed their political opponent to the point of preferring anything to him, even foreign dictatorship. The
French apparently never tire of such potentially fatal
games. They are indeed the strange people who, according to Custine, would rather depict themselves as ugly
than be forgotten. But if their country disappeared, she
would be forgotten, however she had been depicted;
and in a subjugated nation we should not even have the
liberty of continuing to insult each other. Until such
truths are admitted, we must be resigned to giving a
purely personal testimony with all necessary precautions. And, personally, I am interested only in the actions
that here and now can spare useless bloodshed and in
the solutions that guarantee the future of a land whose
suffering I share too much to be able to indulge in
speechmaking about it.

Still other reasons keep me from playing such public
games. To begin with, I lack the assurance that allows

one to settle everything. On this point terrorism as it is practiced in Algeria greatly influenced my attitude. When the fate of men and women of one's own blood is bound, directly or indirectly, to the articles one writes in the comfort of the study, one has a right to hesitate and to weigh the pros and cons. In my case, if I am aware that in criticizing the course of the rebellion I risk justifying the most brazen instigators of the Algerian drama, I never cease fearing that, by pointing out the long series of French mistakes, I may, without running any risk myself, provide an alibi for the insane criminal who may throw his bomb into an innocent crowd that includes my family. I went so far as to admit this fact baldly in a recent declaration which was commented upon most strangely. But anyone who does not know the situation I am talking about can hardly judge of it. And if anyone, knowing it, still thinks heroically that one's brother must die rather than one's principles, I shall go no farther than to admire him from a distance. I am not of his stamp.

This does not mean that principles have no meaning. An opposition of ideas is possible, even with weapons in hand, and it is only fair to recognize one's opponent's reasons even before defending oneself against him. But on both sides a reign of terror, as long as it lasts, changes the scale of values. When one's own family is in immediate danger of death, one may want to instill in one's family a feeling of greater generosity and fairness, as these articles clearly show; but (let there be no doubt about it!) one still feels a natural solidarity with the family in such mortal danger and hopes that it will survive at least and, by surviving, have a chance to show its fairness. If that is not honor and true justice, then I know nothing that is of any use in this world.

Only from such a position have we the right and the duty to state that military combat and repression have, on our side, taken on aspects that we cannot accept. Reprisals against civilian populations and the use of torture are crimes in which we are all involved. The fact that such things could take place among us is a humiliation we must henceforth face. Meanwhile, we must at least refuse to justify such methods, even on the score of efficacy. The moment they are justified, even indirectly, there are no more rules or values; all causes are equally good, and war without aims or laws sanctions the triumph of nihilism. Willy-nilly, we go back in that case to the jungle where the sole principle is violence. Even those who are fed up with morality ought to realize that it is better to suffer certain injustices than to commit them even to win wars, and that such deeds do us more harm than a hundred underground forces on the enemy's side. When excuses are made, for instance, for those who do not hesitate to slaughter the innocent in Algeria or, in other places, to torture or to condone torture, are they not also incalculable errors since they may justify the very crimes we want to fight? And what is that efficacy whereby we manage to justify everything that is most unjustifiable in our adversary? Consequently, the chief argument of those who are trying to make the best of torture must be met head on. Torture has perhaps saved some, at the expense of honor, by uncovering thirty bombs, but at the same time it aroused fifty new terrorists who, operating in some other way and in another place, will cause the death of even more innocent people. Even when accepted in the interest of realism and efficacy, such a flouting of honor serves no purpose but to degrade our country in her own eyes and abroad. Finally, such fine deeds inevitably lead to the demoralization of France and the loss of Algeria. And censorship, always stupid, whether resulting from shame or cynicism, will not change anything about these truths. The government's duty is not to suppress protests, even interested protests, against the criminal excesses of repression. Its duty is rather to suppress the excesses and to condemn them publicly in order to keep each individual citizen from feeling personally responsible for the actions of a few and hence obliged to denounce or approve them.

But, to be both useful and equitable, we must condemn with equal force and in no uncertain terms the terrorism applied by the F.L.N. to French civilians and indeed, to an even greater degree, to Arab civilians. Such terrorism is a crime that can be neither excused nor allowed to develop. Under the form it has assumed, no revolutionary movement has ever accepted it, and the Russian terrorists of 1905, for instance, would have died (they proved this statement) rather than stoop to it. It would be impossible to transform an awareness of the injustices imposed on the Arab population into a systematic indulgence toward those who indiscriminately slaughter Arab and French civilians without regard for age or sex. After all, Gandhi proved that it is possible to fight for one's people and win without for a moment losing the world's respect. Whatever the cause being defended, it will always be dishonored by the blind slaughter of an innocent crowd when the killer knows in advance that he will strike down women and children.

I have never failed to state, as can be seen in these reports, that these two condemnations could not be separated if we wanted to be effective. This is why it seemed to me both indecent and harmful to protest against tortures in the company of those who readily accepted Melouza or the mutilation of European children. Just as it seemed to me harmful and indecent to condemn terrorism in the company of those who are not bothered by torture. The truth, alas, is that a part of French opinion vaguely holds that the Arabs have in a way earned the right to slaughter and mutilate while another part is willing to justify in a way all excesses. To justify himself, each relies on the other's crime. But that is a casuistry of blood, and it strikes me that an intellectual cannot become involved in it, unless he takes up arms himself. When violence answers violence in a growing frenzy that makes the simple language of reason impossible, the role of intellectuals cannot be, as we read every day, to excuse from a distance one of the violences and condemn the other. This has the double result of enraging the violent group that is condemned and encouraging to greater violence the violent group that is exonerated. If they do not join the combatants themselves, their role (less spectacular, to be sure!) must be merely to strive for pacification so that reason will again have a chance. A perspicacious Right, without giving up any of its convictions, would thus have attempted to persuade its members, both in Algeria and in the government, of the necessity for major reforms and of the discreditable nature of certain forms of behavior. An intelligent Left, without giving up any of its principles, would likewise have attempted to persuade the Arab movement that certain methods were essentially base. But not at all. Most often the Right ratified, in the name of French honor, what was most opposed to that honor. And most often the Left, in the name of justice, excused what was an insult to any real justice. In this way the Right abandoned the monopoly of the moral reflex to the Left, which yielded to it the monopoly of the patriotic reflex. The country suffered doubly. We could have used moralists less joyfully resigned to their country's misfortune and patriots less ready to allow torturers to claim that they were acting in the name of France. It seems as if metropolitan France was unable to think of any policies other than those which consisted in saying to the French in Algeria: "Go ahead and die; that's what you deserve" or else "Kill them; that's what they deserve." That makes two different policies and a single abdication, for the question is not how to die separately but rather how to live together.

If I annoy anyone by writing this, I ask him merely to think for a moment about the divergence between the ideological reflexes. Some want their country to identify itself wholly with justice, and they are right. But is it possible to be just and free in a dead or subjugated nation? And does not absolute purity for a nation coincide with historical death? Others want the very body of their country to be defended against the whole universe if need be, and they are not wrong. But is it possible to survive as a people without doing reasonable justice to other peoples? France is dying through inability to solve this dilemma. The first want the universal to the detriment of the particular. The others want the particular to the detriment of the universal. But the two go together. The way to human society passes through national society. National society can be preserved only by opening it up to a universal perspective. More precisely, if you want France alone to reign in Algeria over eight million mutes, she will die. If you want Algeria to separate from France, both of them will perish in the same way. If, on the other hand, French and Arabs resolve their differences in Algeria, the future will have a meaning for the French, the Arabs, and the whole world.

But to achieve that, we must cease looking upon the mass of Arabs in Algeria as a nation of butchers. The great majority of them, exposed on all sides, feel a suffering that no one expresses for them. Millions of men, crazed with poverty and fear, have dug themselves in, and neither Cairo nor Algiers ever speaks up for them. You will see that I have tried for a long time to point out something of their misery, and my somber descriptions will probably be held against me. Yet I wrote complaining of Arab misery when there was still time to do something, at a time when France was strong and when there was silence among those who now find it easier to keep heaping abuse, even abroad, upon their weakened country. If my voice had been more widely heard twenty years ago, there would perhaps be less bloodshed at present. The misfortune (and I feel it to be a misfortune) is that events proved me right. Today the poverty of the Algerian peasants may well increase out of all proportion as a result of a lightning growth in population. In addition, caught between the combatants, they suffer from fear; they too, they above all, need peace! It is of them and of my family that I continue to think as I write the name Algeria and make a plea for reconciliation. They are the ones to whom we must give a voice and a future liberated from fear and hunger.

But to achieve that, we must cease condemning the French in Algeria as a group. One body of opinion in metropolitan France, which insists on hating them, must be called to order. When a French partisan of the F.L.N. dares to write that the French in Algeria have always looked upon France as a prostitute to be exploited, such an irresponsible person must be reminded that he is speaking of men whose grandparents, for instance, decided in favor of France in 1871 and left their Alsatian soil for Algeria, whose fathers died together in the east of France in 1914, and who themselves, twice mobilized in the most recent war, were indefatigable, along with hundreds of thousands of Moslems, in fighting on all fronts for that prostitute. As a result, they can doubtless be considered naïve, but it is hard to call them pimps. I am summing up here the story of the men of my family, who, being poor and free of hatred, never exploited or oppressed anyone. But three quarters of the French in Algeria resemble them and, if only they are provided reasons rather than insults, will be ready to admit the necessity of a juster and freer order. There have doubtless been exploiters in Algeria, but fewer than in metropolitan France, and the first one to benefit from the colonial

system is the entire French nation. If some Frenchmen
consider that, as a result of its colonizing, France (and
France alone among so many holy and pure nations) is
in a state of sin historically, they don't have to point to
the French in Algeria as scapegoats ("Go ahead and
die; that's what we deserve!"); they must offer up themselves in expiation. As far as I am concerned, it seems to
me revolting to beat one's *mea culpa,* as our judge-peni-
tents do, on someone else's breast, useless to condemn
several centuries of European expansion, and absurd to
include in the same denunciation Christopher Colum-
bus and Lyautey. The period of colonialism is over; we
simply have to know this and draw the conclusions. And
the West, which within ten years has granted autonomy
to a dozen colonies, deserves more respect in this regard
and, above all, more patience than Russia, which in the
same period of time has colonized or put under a harsh
protectorate a dozen countries of great and ancient civilization. It is good for a nation to be strong enough in tradition and honor to have the courage to point out its own
mistakes. But it must not forget whatever reasons it still
has for self-esteem. It is dangerous in any case to expect
that a nation will confess that it alone is guilty and to
condemn it to perpetual penance. I believe in a policy of
reparation in Algeria rather than in a policy of expiation.
Problems must be seen in relation to the future, without
endlessly going back over the errors of the past. And
there will be no future that does not do justice at one
and the same time to the two communities of Algeria.

Such a spirit of equity, to be sure, seems alien to the
reality of our history, in which relationships of force out-

line another sort of justice; in our international society
there is no good ethical system except a nuclear ethics.
Then the only guilty one is the vanquished. It is understandable that many intellectuals have consequently
come to the conclusion that values and words derive
their meaning altogether from force. Hence some people
progress without transition from speeches about the principles of honor or fraternity to adoring the *fait accompli* or the cruelest party. I continue, however, to believe,
with regard to Algeria and to everything else, that such
aberrations, both on the Right and on the Left, merely
define the nihilism of our epoch. If it is true that in history, at least, values—whether those of the nation or
those of humanity—do not survive unless they have
been fought for, the fight is not enough to justify them.
The fight itself must rather be justified, and elucidated,
by those values. When fighting for your truth, you must
take care not to kill it with the very arms you are using to
defend it—only under such a double condition do words
resume their living meaning. Knowing that, the intellectual has the role of distinguishing in each camp the
respective limits of force and justice. That role is to clar-
ify definitions in order to disintoxicate minds and to
calm fanaticisms, even when this is against the current
tendency.

I have attempted the work of disintoxication as best I
could. Let us admit that up to now the results have been
nonexistent; these reports are also the record of a failure.
But the simplifications of hatred and prejudice, which
are constantly rotting and reviving the Algerian conflict,
must be noted every day, and one man cannot do so

alone. There would have to be a movement, a press, a ceaseless action. For one ought to note likewise, every day, the lies and omissions that obscure the real problem. Our governments already want to make war without calling it by name, want to have an independent policy and beg money from our allies, and want to invest in Algeria while protecting the standard of living in metropolitan France. They think they can be uncompromising in public and come to terms behind the scenes, covering up the stupidities of their administrators and yet disavowing them in a whisper. But our parties or sects that criticize the government are no more brilliant. No one says clearly what he wants or, if he does so, draws the conclusions. Those who advocate the military solution must know that it can only mean a reconquest by means of an all-out war which will involve, for example, the reconquest of Tunisia in opposition to the opinion, and perhaps the armed resistance, of a part of the world. That is a policy, to be sure, but it must be seen and presented as it is. Those who, in purposely vague terms, advocate negotiation with the F.L.N. cannot fail to be aware, after the precise statements of the F.L.N., that this means the independence of Algeria under the direction of the most relentless military leaders of the insurrection—in other words, the eviction of 1,200,000 Europeans from Algeria and the humiliation of millions of Frenchmen, with all the risks that such a humiliation involves. That is a policy, to be sure, but we must see it for what it is and stop cloaking it in euphemisms.

The constant polemics that would have to be carried on for this purpose would boomerang in a political soci-

ety where the will to be lucid and intellectual independence are becoming rarer and rarer. All that is left of
a hundred articles written on the subject is the adversary's distortion of them. At least a book, if it does not
avoid all misunderstandings, makes some of them impossible.[1] A book can be referred to, and it can present a
calmer statement of the necessary distinctions. Hence,
wanting to satisfy all those who sincerely ask me to state
my position once more, I have been able to do so only by
summing up in this book twenty years of experience,
which may inform unprejudiced minds. By experience I
mean a man's facing up to a situation over a period of
years, with all the mistakes, contradictions, and hesitations that such a confrontation implies, of which many
an example will be found in the following pages. My
opinion, moreover, is that too much is expected of a
writer in such matters. Even, and perhaps especially,
when his birth and his heart link him to the fate of a
land like Algeria, it is useless to think he is blessed with
some kind of revelation of the truth; his personal story, if
it could be truthfully written, would be but the story of
successive lapses, sometimes corrected and committed
once again. I am quite ready to admit my shortcomings
on this score and the errors of judgment that can be noted
in this volume. But, however much it may pain me to do
so, I at least thought it possible to gather together the
documents of this long record and to submit them to the

[1] The entire book entitled *Actuelles III* was devoted to Camus's
"Algerian Reports" of the years 1939–58, from among which he
selected for this volume the present "Preface" and the three
following essays. (Translator's note)

reflection of those whose minds are not yet irrevocably made up. The relaxation of psychological strain that can be felt at present between French and Arabs in Algeria gives rise to the hope that the language of reason may again be heard.

Consequently, there will be found in these records a picture (on the occasion of a very serious crisis in Kabylia) of the economic causes of the Algerian drama, a few references for the specifically political evolution of that drama, comments on the complexity of the present situation, a prediction of the impasse to which the revival of terrorism and repression has led us, and, in conclusion, an outline of the solution that still seems to me possible. Recognizing the end of colonialism, my solution excludes dreams of reconquest or of maintaining the *status quo;* really mere reactions of weakness and humiliation, such dreams only prepare for the definitive divorce and the double misfortune of France and Algeria. But my solution also excludes the dream of uprooting the French in Algeria, who, if they haven't the right to oppress anyone, do have the right not to be oppressed and to be their own masters in the land of their birth. There are other ways of re-establishing the necessary justice than substituting one injustice for another.

In this regard I have tried to define my position clearly. An Algeria made up of federated settlements and linked to France seems to me preferable (without any possible comparison on the plane of simple justice) to an Algeria linked to an empire of Islam which would bring the Arab peoples only increased poverty and suffering and which would tear the Algerian-born French from their natural home. If the Algeria I hope for still has a chance of emerging (and, in my opinion, it has many chances), I want to help it with all my strength. On the other hand, I consider that I must not help even for a second in any way whatever the establishment of the other Algeria. If it came about (and, necessarily, against the interests of France or without consideration for France), through the joint operation of the forces of surrender and the forces of pure conservation (with the double retreat they involve), this would be a great misfortune for me, and, with millions of other Frenchmen, I should have to suffer the consequences. That, loyally stated, is what I think. I may be mistaken or unable to judge fairly of a drama that touches me too closely. But if the reasonable hopes we can still nourish today should fade away and we were faced with the serious ensuing events for which—whether they do violence to our country or to humanity as a whole—we shall all be responsible together, each of us must stand up and declare what he has done and what he has said. This is my declaration, to which I shall add nothing.

March–April 1958

LETTER TO
AN ALGERIAN MILITANT

(M. Aziz Kessous, an Algerian socialist and former member of the Party of the Manifesto, had planned, after the rebellion broke out, to launch a newspaper, *Algerian Community*, which would rise above the double fanaticism now afflicting Algeria and help establish a really free community. This letter appeared in the newspaper's first issue on the first of October 1955.)

MY DEAR KESSOUS,
I found your letters on returning from a vacation and am afraid that my approval may come very late. Yet I need to give it to you. Believe me when I tell you that Algeria is the cause of my suffering at present as others might say their chest is the cause of their suffering. And since the 20th of August I have been on the verge of despair.

We know nothing of the human heart if we imagine that the Algerian French can now forget the massacres at

Philippeville and elsewhere. And it is another form of madness to imagine that repression can make the Arab masses feel confidence and esteem for France. Hence we are pitted against each other, condemned to inflicting the greatest possible pain on each other, inexpiably. The idea is intolerable to me and poisons each of my days.

Nevertheless, you and I, who are so much alike—having the same background, sharing the same hope, having felt like brothers for so long now, united in our love for our country—know that we are not enemies and that we could live happily together on this soil that belongs to us. For it is ours, and I can no more imagine it without you and your brothers than you can probably separate it from me and those who resemble me.

You have said it very well, better than I can say it: we are condemned to live together. The Algerian French—and I thank you for having pointed out that they are not all bloodthirsty rich men—have been in Algeria for more than a century, and there are more than a million of them. This alone is enough to distinguish the Algerian problem from the problems raised in Tunisia and Morocco, where the French settlement is relatively new and weak. The "French fact" cannot be eliminated in Algeria, and the dream of a sudden disappearance of France is childish. But there is no reason either why nine million Arabs should live on their land like forgotten men; the dream that the Arab masses can be canceled out, silenced and subjugated, is just as mad. The French are attached to the soil of Algeria by roots that are too old and too vigorous for us to think of tearing them up. But this gives the French no right, in my opinion, to destroy the roots of Arab culture and life. Throughout my life I have fought for sweeping and profound reforms—and you know that I paid for this with exile from my country. But people refused to believe because they cherished the dream of power that is supposedly eternal and forgot that history constantly progresses; and now those reforms are needed more than ever. Those which you point out represent an initial effort, and an indispensable one, to be made quickly, before its chance of success is drowned in French blood and Arab blood.

But saying this today, as I know by experience, amounts to taking one's stand in the no man's land between two armies and preaching amid the bullets that war is a deception and that bloodshed, if it sometimes makes history progress, makes it progress toward even greater barbarism and misery. If anyone dares to put his whole heart and all his suffering into such a cry, he will hear in reply nothing but laughter and a louder clash of arms. And yet we must cry it aloud, and, since you plan to do so, I cannot let you do such a mad and necessary thing without telling you that I stand beside you like a brother.

Yes, the essential thing is to leave room, however limited it may be, for the exchange of views that is still possible; the essential thing is to bring about an easing of the situation, however slight and temporary it may be. And to achieve that, each of us must preach pacification to his people. The inexcusable massacring of French civilians leads to equally stupid destruction of the Arabs and their possessions. It is as if two insane people, crazed with wrath, had decided to turn into a fatal embrace the forced marriage from which they cannot free themselves. Forced to live together and incapable of uniting, they decide at least to die together. And because each of them by his excesses strengthens the motives and excesses of the other, the storm of death that has struck our country can only increase to the point of general destruction. In that ceaseless attempt to go one better, the fire is spreading, and tomorrow Algeria will be a land of ruins and dead which no force, no power in the world, will be capable of reviving in this century.

We must put a stop to the attempt at outbidding each other; it is the duty of all of us, Arabs and Frenchmen, who refuse to let go each other's hands. We Frenchmen must struggle to keep repression from becoming general so that French law will continue to have a generous and obvious meaning in our country; we must struggle to remind our people of their mistakes and of the obligations of a great nation, which cannot, without losing its prestige, answer a racial massacre with a similar outburst. Finally, we must strive to hasten the necessary and decisive reforms that will once more launch the Franco-Arab community of Algeria on the road toward the future. You Arabs must spare no effort to show your people that, when they kill civilian populations, terrorism not only raises justifiable doubts as to the political maturity of men capable of such acts, but also strengthens the anti-Arab elements, reinforces their arguments, and silences French liberal opinion which might find and put through some solution leading to reconciliation.

I shall be told, as you will be told, that it is too late for reconciliation, that the only thing to do is to wage war

and win. But you and I know that this war will not have
any real victors and that, once it is over, we shall still
have to go on living together forever on the same soil.
We know that our destinies are so closely linked that
any action on the part of one calls forth a retort from the
other, crime engendering crime, madness replying to
lunacy, and, finally, that if one stands aloof the other
suffers from sterility. If you Arab democrats fail in your
work of pacification, the activity of us French liberals
will be doomed to failure in advance. And if we falter in
our duty, your poor words will be swept away in the
wind and flames of a pitiless war.

This is why I am with you in your effort, my dear Kessous. I wish you, I wish us, luck. I want most earnestly to
believe that peace will rise over our fields, our mountains, our shores, and that then at last Arabs and French,
reconciled in freedom and justice, will make an effort to
forget the bloodshed that divides them today. When that
happens, we who are both exiled in hatred and despair
shall together recover our native land.

APPEAL FOR A
CIVILIAN TRUCE IN ALGERIA

(Lecture given in Algiers in
February 1956)

LADIES and gentlemen, despite the need to sur-
round this meeting with precautions, despite
the difficulties we have encountered, I shall speak this
evening not to divide but to unite. That is my most ar-
dent wish. Not the least of my disappointments (and
the expression is weak) is to have to admit that everything stands in the way of such a wish. For instance, a
man and writer who has devoted a part of his life to
serving Algeria is almost deprived of the right to speak,
even before anyone knows what he intends to say. But
at the same time this emphasizes the urgency of the effort toward pacification that we must make. Consequently, this meeting had to take place to show at least
that an exchange of views is still possible and to keep
people from accepting the worst as a result of the general discouragement.

My speaking of "an exchange of views" suggests that
I did not come to deliver a formal lecture. To tell the
truth, in the present circumstances I should not have the
heart to do so. But it seemed to me possible, and I even
considered it my duty, to come and echo among you a

purely humanitarian appeal that might, at least on one
point, silence the fury and unite most Algerians, both
French and Arab, without their having to give up any of
their convictions. That appeal, endorsed by the committee that organized this meeting, is addressed to both
camps in the hope that they will accept a truce insofar
as innocent civilians are concerned.

Hence I have only to justify such an enterprise in
your eyes. I shall try to do so briefly.

Let me insist at the outset that, owing to the force of
circumstances, our appeal has nothing to do with politics. If it were otherwise, I should not be qualified to
speak. I am not a political man, and my passions and
inclinations do not lead me to public platforms. I step
onto the podium only when forced to by the pressure of
circumstances and by my conception of my function as a
writer. As to the basis of the Algerian problem, I shall
probably have, as events multiply and suspicions increase on both sides, more doubts than certainties to express. My only qualifications for taking a stand are that
I have lived through the Algerian calamity as a personal
tragedy and that I am incapable of rejoicing over any
death whatever. For twenty years, with paltry means, I
have done all I could to contribute to the understanding
of our two peoples. To be sure, one can laugh at the expression of the preacher of reconciliation when history
answers his preaching by showing him the two peoples
he loved embraced in a death grip. He himself, in any
case, is not inclined to laugh at it. Faced with such a
failure, his only concern must be to spare his country
any unnecessary suffering.

I must add that the men who took the initiative of
backing this appeal are not acting in any political capacity either. Among them are members of large religious
families who were willing, in keeping with their lofty
calling, to support a humanitarian duty. Others are men
not singled out either by profession or by sensitivity as
the kind who get involved in public affairs. For most of
them, indeed, their profession or business, which served
a purpose in the community, sufficed to fill their lives.
They could have stood on the sidelines, like so many
others, keeping score and from time to time sighing
with a fine note of melancholy. But they thought that
building, teaching, creating were functions of life and
of generosity which could not be pursued in the realm
of hatred and bloodshed. Such a decision, heavy with
consequences and commitments, gives them no special
rights except one—the right of asking that their sugges-
tion be seriously considered.

I must say finally that we don't want to get you to
agree to anything politically. If we wanted to raise the
problem on a political basis, we should run the risk of
not getting the agreement we need. We may differ as to
the necessary solutions and even as to the means of
achieving them. To contrast positions that have been defined over and over and even distorted would, for the
moment, merely add to the weight of insults and hatreds
under which our country is stifling and struggling.

But one thing at least unites all of us—and that is our
love of our common soil, and our anguish. Anguish as
we face a future that closes up a little every day, as we
face the threat of a degrading struggle, of an economic

disequilibrium that is already serious and is increasing every day, that may reach the point where no effort will be able to revive Algeria for a long time to come.

We want to address ourselves to that anguish, even— I might say, especially—among those who have already taken sides. For even among the most militant, in the thick of the fray, there is an element, I know, that will not indulge in murder and hatred, and that dreams of a happy Algeria.

We are appealing to that element in each of you, French or Arab. We should like to say to those who are unwilling to see this great country break in two and go adrift that, without recalling again the mistakes of the past, anxious solely for the future, it is possible today, on a single definite point, to agree first and then to save human lives. In this way we may prepare a climate more favorable to a discussion that will at last be reasonable. The intentional modesty of this objective, and yet its importance, make it worthy, in my opinion, of your broadest agreement.

What do we want? Simply to get the Arab movement and the French authorities, without having to make contact or to commit themselves to anything else, to declare simultaneously that for the duration of the fighting the civilian population will on every occasion be respected and protected. Why this measure? The first reason, on which I shall not insist much, is, as I said, one of simple humanity. Whatever the ancient and deep origins of the Algerian tragedy, one fact remains: no cause justifies the death of the innocent. Throughout history, men, unable to suppress war, have made an effort to limit its effects; and, however terrible and repulsive the latest world wars were, nevertheless organizations of aid and solidarity succeeded in piercing the darkness with the feeble ray of pity that keeps one from despairing utterly of mankind. Such a necessity seems even more urgent in a struggle that in many ways has the appearance of a fratricidal war that makes no distinction between men and women, between soldier and worker. From this point of view, even if our present initiative saved but one innocent life, it would be justified.

But it is also justified for other reasons. However black it may seem, the future of Algeria is not yet altogether sealed. If each individual, Arab or French, made an effort to think over his adversary's motives, at least the basis of a fruitful discussion would be clear. But if the two Algerian populations, each accusing the other of having begun the quarrel, were to hurl themselves against each other in a sort of xenophobic madness, then any chance for understanding would be drowned in blood. It may be, and this is our greatest source of anguish, that we are heading toward such horrors. But we Arabs and French who reject mad, nihilistic destruction cannot let this happen without launching a final appeal to reason.

Reason clearly shows that on this point, at least, French and Arab solidarity is inevitable, in death as in life, in destruction as in hope. The frightful aspect of that solidarity is apparent in the infernal dialectic that whatever kills one side kills the other too, each blaming the other and justifying his violences by the opponent's violence. The eternal question as to who was first responsible loses all meaning then. And because they could not manage to live together, two populations, similar and different at the same time but equally worthy of respect, are condemned to die together, with rage in their hearts.

But there is also a community of hope that justifies our appeal. That common hope is firmly based on realities over which we have no control. On this soil there are a million Frenchmen who have been here for a century, millions of Moslems, either Arabs or Berbers, who have been here for centuries, and several vigorous religious communities. Those men must live together at the crossroads where history put them. They can do so if they will take a few steps toward each other in an open confrontation. Then our differences ought to help us instead of dividing us. As for me, here as in every domain, I believe only in differences and not in uniformity. First of all, because differences are the roots without which the tree of liberty, the sap of creation and of civilization, dries up. Nevertheless, we stand facing each other as if frozen, as if struck with a paralysis that can be cured only by brutal and brief outbursts of violence. This is because the struggle has assumed an irrevocable aspect that rouses on both sides towering indignations and passions aspiring to outdo each other.

"No further discussion is possible"—that is the slogan that sterilizes any future and any possibility of life. After that there is nothing but blind warfare in which the Frenchman makes up his mind to know nothing of the Arab, even though he feels, somewhere within him, that the Arab's claim to dignity is justified, and the Arab

makes up his mind to know nothing of the Frenchman,
even though he feels, somewhere within him, that the
Algerian French likewise have a right to security and
dignity on our common soil. Locked up in his rancor and
hatred, neither one can listen to the other. Any proposal,
whichever side it comes from, is received with distrust,
distorted at once and made unserviceable. We are gradually getting caught in a tangle of old and new accusations, of fixed vendettas, of relentless rancors alternating
with one another. It's like an old family lawsuit in which
grievances and arguments pile up for generations until
even the most humane and upright judges can make
neither head nor tail of the matter. It is hard to imagine
the end of such a situation, and our hope for a Franco-
Arabic association, for a peaceful and creative Algeria,
becomes dimmer every day.

Consequently, if we want to preserve some of that
hope, at least until discussion about the fundamentals
gets under way, if we want to help such a discussion get
somewhere by making a joint effort toward understanding, we must act upon the very character of the struggle.
We are too much hampered by the scope of the drama
and the complexity of the passions it has loosed to hope
to achieve a cessation of hostilities at once. Such an action would indeed imply the taking of purely political
positions which, at the moment, might divide us even
more.

But we can at least exert some action on the most hateful aspect of the fight: we can propose, without making
any change in the present situation, that we refrain from
what makes it unforgivable—the murder of the inno-

cent. The fact that such an agreement would unite French and Arabs, both of them eager not to cause irreparable suffering, would give it a serious chance of succeeding in both camps.

If our proposal had a chance of being accepted—and it does have such a chance—we should not only have saved precious human lives but also have re-created a proper climate for a healthy discussion that would not be spoiled by ridiculously uncompromising attitudes; we should have prepared the ground for a fairer, subtler understanding of the Algerian problem. By bringing about such a slight thaw on a single point, we may hope someday to break altogether the block of hatreds and crazy demands in which we are all caught. Then the various policies would have a hearing and each individual would again have the right to defend his own convictions and to explain his difference.

That, in any case, is the narrow position on which we may hope, as a beginning, to get together. Any broader platform would, for the moment, provide us only an additional field of discord. We must be patient with ourselves.

But I do not believe that any Frenchman or any Arab would refuse to agree to such limited and yet capital action. To convince ourselves of this we have only to imagine what would happen if this enterprise, cautious and limited as it is, were to fail. We should have to face a definitive break, the destruction of all hope, and a carnage of which we have so far had only a slight foretaste. Those of our Arab friends who courageously stand beside us in the no man's land where we are threatened on both sides and who are torn within themselves would be forced to adopt a policy of retaliation that would kill all possibility of free discussion. The essential dialogue between us could not take place. Directly or indirectly, they would enter the fray, whereas they could have been artisans of peace. Every Frenchman's interest, therefore, is to help them escape such a dilemma.

But, on the other hand, the direct interest of Arab moderates is to help us escape another dilemma. For if we fail in our undertaking and give proof of our impotence, the French liberals who think that French and Arabs can be made to coexist, who believe that such coexistence will do justice to the rights of both sides, who are sure in any case that it alone can save the people of this country from calamity, will be given the lie.

Instead of the broad community they long for, they will have to fall back on the only living community that justifies them—France. In other words, by our silence or by the stand we take, we too shall enter the fray. I cannot speak in the name of our Arab friends to illustrate both sides of that fearful evolution which gives an urgency to our action. But I have seen how possible such an evolution is in France. Just as I have felt here the Arab's distrust of whatever is proposed to him, one can feel in France, as you are well aware, a growing doubt and similar distrust. The doubt and distrust may become permanent if the French, already disturbed by the continuation of the Rif war after the Sultan's return and by the revival of the Fellagha movement in Tunisia, are forced by the spread of a relentless struggle to think that the aim of the struggle is not only the Arab claim to

justice but also the achievement of foreign ambitions—
at the expense of France and her complete ruin. Many
Frenchmen would then indulge in reasoning exactly as
the majority of Arabs would reason if, losing all hope,
they had to accept the inevitable. The French reasoning
would run like this: "We are French. Regard for what is
just in the cause of our adversaries will not lead us to do
injustice to everything good and deserving in France
and her people. We cannot be expected to applaud all
forms of nationalism except French nationalism, to forgive all sins except those of France. In the extremity to
which we have been driven and since a choice is necessary, we cannot choose anything else but our own country."

Thus, through the same reasoning operating in contrary directions, our two peoples would separate once
and for all and Algeria would become for a long time a
mass of ruins, whereas a mere effort of reflection today
could still change things and avoid catastrophe.

This is the double danger that threatens us, the mortal
risk with which we are faced. Either we shall succeed,
on one point at least, in getting together to limit the
havoc and shall in this way bring about a satisfactory
outcome, or we shall fail to unite and to persuade—
and our failure will influence the whole future. Our
enterprise needs no other justification; the urgency is
evident. This is why my appeal will be as emphatic as
possible. If I had the power to give a voice to the solitude and anguish in each of us, that is the voice with
which I should address you. As for me, I have passionately loved this land where I was born, I drew from it

whatever I am, and in forming friendships I have never made any distinction among the men who live here, whatever their race. Although I have known and shared every form of poverty in which this country abounds, it is for me the land of happiness, of energy, and of creation. And I cannot bear to see it become a land of suffering and hatred.

I know that the great tragedies of history often fascinate men with approaching horror. Paralyzed, they cannot make up their minds to do anything but wait. So they wait, and one day the Gorgon devours them. But I should like to convince you that the spell can be broken, that there is only an illusion of impotence, that strength of heart, intelligence, and courage are enough to stop fate and sometimes reverse it. One has merely to will this, not blindly, but with a firm and reasoned will.

People are too readily resigned to fatality. They are too ready to believe that, after all, nothing but bloodshed makes history progress and that the stronger always progresses at the expense of the weaker. Such fatality exists perhaps. But man's task is not to accept it or to bow to its laws. If he had accepted it in the earliest ages, we should still be living in prehistoric times. The task of men of culture and faith, in any case, is not to desert historical struggles nor to serve the cruel and inhuman elements in those struggles. It is rather to remain what they are, to help man against what is oppressing him, to favor freedom against the fatalities that close in upon it.

That is the condition under which history really progresses, innovates—in a word, creates. In everything else it repeats itself, like a bleeding mouth that merely vomits forth a wild stammering. Today we are at the stage of stammering, and yet the broadest perspectives are opening up for our century. We are at the stage of a duel with daggers, or almost, while the world is progressing at the speed of supersonic planes. The same day that our newspapers print the dreadful story of our provincial squabbles, they announce the European atomic pool. Tomorrow, if only Europe can come to an internal agreement, floods of riches will cover the continent and, overflowing even to us, will make our problems out of date and our hatreds null and void.

For that still unimaginable but not so distant future we must organize and stand together. The absurd and heart-breaking aspect of the tragedy we are living through comes out in the fact that, in order someday to reach those world-wide perspectives, we must now gather together in paltry fashion to beg merely, without making any other claims yet, that on a single spot of the globe a handful of innocent victims be spared. But since that is our task, however obscure and ungrateful it may be, we must tackle it decisively in order to deserve living someday as free men—in other words, as men who refuse either to practice or to suffer terror.

ALGERIA 1958

(For the sake of those who still ask me what future can be expected for Algeria, I have attempted, in the shortest possible space and staying as close as possible to the Algerian reality, to draw up a brief statement.)

I F THE Arab demands, as they are expressed today, were altogether legitimate, it is probable that Algeria would now be autonomous, with the approval of French opinion. If that opinion nonetheless accepts war and, even among Communists or Communist sympathizers, is limited to platonic protests, this is because, among other reasons, the Arab demands are equivocal. That ambiguity, and the confused reactions it arouses among our governments and throughout the country, explains the ambiguity of the French reaction, the omissions and the uncertainties the French use as an excuse. The first thing to do is to bring some clarity to those demands in order to try to frame clearly the reply that should be made.

A. What is legitimate in the Arab demands.

They are right, and every Frenchman knows this, to point out and reject:

1) Colonialism and its abuses, which are man-made.

2) The perennial lie of constantly proposed but
never realized assimilation, a lie that has compromised
every evolution since the establishment of colonialism.
The faked elections of 1948 in particular both illustrated
the lie and utterly discouraged the Arab people. Until
that date the Arabs all wanted to be French. After that
date a large part of them no longer wanted to be.

3) The obvious injustice of the agrarian allocation
and of the distribution of income (sub-proletariat)—
injustices that are, moreover, being irreparably aggravated by a rapid increase in population.

4) The psychological suffering: the often scornful or
offhand manner of many French, and the development
among the Arabs (through a series of stupid measures)
of the complex of humiliation that is at the center of the
present drama.

The events of 1945 should have been a warning signal; the pitiless repression of the area around Constan-
tine, on the contrary, emphasized the anti-French movement. The French authorities judged that such repression put an end to the rebellion. In fact, it gave the
rebellion a starting signal.

It is beyond doubt that the Arab demands on all these
points, which in part summed up the historic condition
of the Arabs of Algeria until 1948, are thoroughly legitimate. The injustice from which the Arab population
has suffered is linked to colonialism itself, to its history
and its administration. The French central power has
never been in a position to make French law dominate
in its colonies. It is beyond doubt, in short, that signal

amends must be made to the Algerian people which will restore to them both dignity and justice.

B. What is illegitimate in the Arab demands.

The wish to recover a life of dignity and freedom, the total loss of confidence in any political solution guaranteed by France, the romanticism too that is natural to very young insurgents without political background have combined to lead certain combatants and their general staff to call for national independence. However well disposed one may be toward the Arab demands, one has to admit that, as far as Algeria is concerned, national independence is a conception springing wholly from emotion. There has never yet been an Algerian nation. The Jews, the Turks, the Greeks, the Italians, the Berbers would have just as much right to claim the direction of that virtual nation. At present the Arabs do not alone make up all of Algeria. The size and seniority of the French settlement, in particular, are enough to create a problem that cannot be compared to anything in history. The Algerian French are likewise, and in the strongest meaning of the word, natives. It must be added that a purely Arab Algeria could not achieve the economic independence without which political independence is but a deception. However inadequate the French effort may be, it is so far-reaching that no country, at the present moment, would be willing to take over. For this question and the problems it raises, I refer the reader to Germaine Tillion's admirable book.[1]

[1] *Algeria: The Realities* (New York: Alfred A. Knopf; 1958).

The Arabs can at least claim kinship, not in a nation,[2] but in a sort of Moslem empire, either spiritual or temporal. Spiritually that empire exists, its adhesive force and doctrine being Islam. But there also exists a Christian empire, at least as important, which there is no question of bringing back as such into temporal history. For the moment, the Arab empire does not exist except in the writings of Colonel Nasser, and it could not come about without world-wide upheavals that would mean the Third World War in a short time. The claims for Algerian national independence must be seen in part as one of the manifestations of this new Arab imperialism in which Egypt, overestimating its strength, aims to take the lead and which, for the moment, Russia is using for its anti-Western strategy. The Russian strategy, which can be read on every map of the globe, consists in calling for the *status quo* in Europe (in other words, the recognition of its own colonial system) and in fomenting trouble in the Middle East and Africa to encircle Europe on the south. The happiness and freedom of the Arab populations are of little account in the whole affair. One has only to think of the slaughter of the Chechenzes or of the Tartars in the Crimea or of the destruction of the Arab culture in the once Moslem provinces of Daghestan. Russia merely takes advantage of such dreams of empire to serve her own designs. Those nationalistic or, in the strictest sense of the word, imperialistic claims must in any case be responsible for the unacceptable as-

[2] The Syrian "nation," the moment it got out from under the French protectorate, melted away, like sugar in water, in Nasser's Arab Republic.

pects of the Arab rebellion—chiefly, the systematic murder of French civilians and Arab civilians killed without
discrimination and solely because they were French or
friends of the French.

Consequently, we are faced with ambiguous demands, which we can approve as to their basic causes
and as to some of their formulations, but which we can
in no manner accept in certain of their developments.
The mistake of the French government from the beginning was never to make any distinctions and consequently never to speak out clearly, and this justified
every form of skepticism and retaliation on the part of
the Arab masses. The result was to strengthen the ex-
tremist and nationalist factions on both sides.

The only chance of getting somewhere with the problem, today as yesterday, is therefore to speak clearly. If
the elements of the problem are:

1) The amends that must be made to eight million
Arabs who have lived until now under a particular form
of oppression;

2) The right of 1,200,000 autochthonous French
people to exist, and to exist in their native land without
ever again being subjected to the discretion of fanatical
military leaders;

3) The strategic interests that condition the freedom
of the West:
then the French government must make it clearly
known:

1) That it is ready to grant complete justice to the
Arabs of Algeria and to liberate them from the colonial
system;

2) That it will give up none of the rights of the Algerian French;

3) That it is unwilling for such justice to mean a prelude to a sort of historical death for the French nation, and for the West the risk of an encircling that would lead to the Kadarization of Europe and the isolation of America.

Hence it is possible to imagine a solemn declaration addressed exclusively to the Arabs and their representatives (it is worth noticing that since the beginning of hostilities no French chief of state or any governor has spoken directly to the Arab population) proclaiming:

1) That the era of colonialism is over, and that France (without blaming herself any more than other nations that grew up at the same time) admits her past and present mistakes and declares herself ready to make amends;

2) That she refuses, however, to yield to violence, especially the forms it assumes at present in Algeria; that she refuses, in particular, to serve the dream of the Arab empire at her own expense, at the expense of the European population of Algeria, and, finally, at the expense of the peace of the world;

3) That she therefore proposes a regime of free association in which every Arab, on the basis of the Lauriol plan,[3] will truly find the privileges of a free citizen.

Of course, the difficulties begin here. But they may never be solved if this preliminary declaration is not solemnly made and directed (as I have said) toward the Arab population by every means of diffusion that a great

[3] See p. 149.

nation possesses. That declaration would doubtless be heard by the Arab masses, who are today tired and disoriented, and, on the other hand, would reassure a large part of the Algerian French by keeping them from blindly opposing the structural reforms that are indispensable.

It remains to define the solution that might be suggested.

New Algeria

The only regime that, in the present state of affairs, would do justice to all parts of the population has long seemed to me to be a federation based on institutions similar to those of the Swiss confederation, which make it possible for different nationalities to live in peace. But I think that an even more original system must be devised. Switzerland is made up of different populations living in different territories. Its institutions aim simply to articulate the political life of its cantons. Algeria, on the other hand, offers the very rare example of different populations overlapping in the same territory. Hence it is essential to associate without fusing together (since federation is to begin with the union of differences), not different territories, but communities with different personalities. The solution proposed by M. Marc Lauriol, Professor of Law at Algiers (even without approving all his *whereases*) seems to me in this regard particularly adapted to Algerian realities and likely to satisfy the need for justice and freedom felt by all the communities.

In the main, his plan combines the advantages of integration and federalism. He proposes, on the one hand, to respect particularisms and, on the other, to associate the two populations in the administration of their common interest. For this purpose he suggests creating, in a first stage, two sections in the French Parliament, a metropolitan section and a Moslem section. The first would include those elected in metropolitan France and by the overseas French and the second would include the Moslems adhering to the Koran. The rule of proportionality would be strictly respected in the election. Thus it is probable that, in a Parliament made up of six hundred Deputies, there would be about fifteen Algerian French representatives and some hundred Moslems. The Moslem section would deliberate separately on all questions involving Moslems and on them alone. The Parliament in full session, including both French and Moslems, would have authority over everything concerning the two communities (for instance, taxation and the budget) or the two communities and metropolitan France (for instance, national defense). The other matters, insofar as they involved only metropolitan France (in civil law particularly) would fall under the exclusive authority of the metropolitan section. Hence laws involving only the Moslems would be the work of the Moslem Deputies alone; laws applying to all would be the work of all; and laws applying solely to the French would be the work of the French Deputies alone. Still in that initial stage, in other words, the government would be responsible to each section or to the two together according to the nature of the questions raised.

During a second stage, after the trial period necessary

to a general reconciliation, it would be essential to draw conclusions from such an innovation. In fact, contrary to all our practices, contrary above all to the deep-rooted prejudices inherited from the French Revolution, we should thus have sanctioned within the republic two equal but distinct categories of citizens. From one point of view, this would mark a sort of revolution against the regime of centralization and abstract individualism resulting from 1789, which, in so many ways, now deserves to be called *"Ancien Régime."* M. Lauriol is right, in any case, to declare that this is nothing less than the birth of a French federal structure that will create a true French Commonwealth.[4] Such institutions must by nature fit into a system that could include the countries of the Magrab and those of black Africa. An Algerian regional Assembly would then express whatever was peculiar to Algeria, while a federal Senate, in which Algeria would be represented, would hold legislative power for everything (army and foreign affairs, for example) involving the whole federation and would elect a responsible federal government. It is essential to see that this system will not be incompatible with the European institutions that may come into being in the future.

This, in any case, should be the French proposal, which would then be maintained permanently until a cease-fire is achieved. That cease-fire is at present made more difficult by the uncompromising attitude of the F.L.N. Their uncompromising attitude is in part spon-

[4] *Le Fédéralisme et l'Algérie* (La Fédération, 9, rue Auber, Paris).

taneous and unrealistic and in part inspired and cynical.
Insofar as it is spontaneous, it can be understood and
an attempt can be made to neutralize it by a really constructive proposal. Insofar as it is inspired from the
outside, it is unacceptable. Under foreign prompting,
independence can be achieved only by a refusal of any
kind of negotiation and a challenge to the worst kind of
warfare. France has no alternative, in this case, but to
continue maintaining the proposal of which I have
spoken, to get it approved by international opinion and
by ever larger segments of Arab opinion, and to try to
get it gradually accepted.

It is possible to imagine something like this for the immediate future. This solution is not utopian as far as Algerian realities are concerned. It is made uncertain only
by the state of French political society. It presupposes in
fact:

1) A collective will in metropolitan France, and particularly acceptance of a policy of austerity that would
have to be borne by the rich (the wage-earners already
bear all the brunt of a scandalously unjust system of
taxation);

2) A government that will reform the Constitution
(which, by the way, has been approved by only a mi-
nority of the French) and that is willing or able to in-
augurate the long, ambitious, and tenacious policy leading to a French federation.

These two conditions may make an objective observer
skeptical. Yet the appearance in France and Algeria of
new and considerable forces, in men and material re-

sources, justifies hope of a rebirth. As a result, such a solution as the one just outlined has a chance of winning out. If not, Algeria will be lost and the consequences will be dreadful for the Arabs and for the French. This is the last warning that a writer who for twenty years has been devoted to the service of Algeria feels he can voice before resuming his silence.

HUNGARY

KADAR HAD HIS DAY OF FEAR

The Hungarian Minister of State Marosan, whose name sounds like a program, declared a few days ago that there would be no further counter-revolution in Hungary. For once, one of Kadar's Ministers has told the truth. How could there be a counter-revolution since it has already seized power? There can be no other revolution in Hungary.

I AM not one of those who long for the Hungarian people to take up arms again in an uprising doomed to be crushed under the eyes of an international society that will spare neither applause nor virtuous tears before returning to their slippers like football enthusiasts on Saturday evening after a big game. There are already too many dead in the stadium, and we can be generous only with our own blood. Hungarian blood has proved to be so valuable to Europe and to freedom that we must try to spare every drop of it.

But I am not one to think there can be even a resigned

or provisional compromise with a reign of terror that
has as much right to be called socialist as the executioners of the Inquisition had to be called Christians.
And, on this anniversary of liberty, I hope with all my
strength that the mute resistance of the Hungarian people will continue, grow stronger, and, echoed by all the
voices we can give it, get unanimous international opinion to boycott its oppressors. And if that opinion is too
flabby or selfish to do justice to a martyred people, if our
voices also are too weak, I hope that the Hungarian resistance will continue until the counter-revolutionary
state collapses everywhere in the East under the weight
of its lies and its contradictions.

The Bloody and Monotonous Rites

For it is indeed a counter-revolutionary state. What else
can we call a regime that forces the father to inform on
his son, the son to demand the supreme punishment for
his father, the wife to bear witness against her husband
—that has raised denunciation to the level of a virtue?
Foreign tanks, police, twenty-year-old girls hanged,
committees of workers decapitated and gagged, scaffolds,
writers deported and imprisoned, the lying press, camps,
censorship, judges arrested, criminals legislating, and
the scaffold again—is this socialism, the great celebration of liberty and justice?

No, we have known, we still know this kind of
thing; these are the bloody and monotonous rites of the
totalitarian religion! Hungarian socialism is in prison or
in exile today. In the palaces of the State, armed to the

teeth, slink the petty tyrants of absolutism, terrified by the very word "liberty," maddened by the word "truth"! The proof is that today, the 15th of March, a day of invincible truth and liberty for all Hungarians, was for Kadar simply a long day of fear.

For many years, however, those tyrants, aided in the West by accomplices who were not obliged by anything or anyone to show such zeal, cloaked their true actions in a heavy smoke screen. When something could be seen through the screen, they or their Western interpreters explained to us that everything would be all right in ten generations or so, that meanwhile everyone was joyfully heading toward the future, that the deported had made the mistake of getting in the way of traffic on the magnificent road of progress, that the executed agreed completely as to their own suppression, that the intellectuals declared themselves delighted with their pretty gag because it was dialectical, and that the proletariat were charmed with their own work because, if they worked overtime for wretched wages, this was in the proper direction of history.

Alas, the people themselves spoke up! They began to talk in Berlin, in Czechoslovakia, in Poznan, and eventually in Budapest. All at once, everywhere, intellectuals tore off their gags. And together, with a single voice, they said that instead of progress there was regression, that the killings had been useless, the deportations useless, the enslavements useless, and that henceforth, to be sure of making real progress, truth and liberty had to be granted to all.

Thus, with the first shout of insurrection in free

Budapest, learned and shortsighted philosophies, miles
of false reasonings and deceptively beautiful doctrines
were scattered like dust. And the truth, the naked truth,
so long outraged, burst upon the eyes of the world.

Contemptuous teachers, unaware that they were
thereby insulting the working classes, had assured us
that the masses could readily get along without liberty
if only they were given bread. And the masses themselves suddenly replied that they didn't have bread but
that, even if they did, they would still like something
else. For it was not a learned professor but a Budapest
blacksmith who wrote: "I want to be considered an adult
eager to think and capable of thought. I want to be able
to express my thoughts without having anything to fear
and I want, also, to be listened to."

As for the intellectuals who had been told and shouted
at that there was no truth other than the one that served
the cause, this is the oath they took at the grave of their
comrades assassinated by that cause: "Never again, not
even under threat and torture, nor under a misunderstood love of the cause, will anything but the truth issue from our mouths." (Tibor Meray at the grave of
Rajk.)

The Scaffold Does Not Become Any More Liberal

After that, the case is closed. The slaughtered people are
our people. What Spain was for us twenty years ago
Hungary will be today. The subtle distinctions, the verbal tricks, and the clever considerations with which people still try to cloak the truth do not interest us. The com-

petition we are told about between Rakosi and Kadar is unimportant. The two are of the same stamp. They differ only by the number of heads to their credit, and if Rakosi's total is more impressive, this will not be so for long.

In any event, whether the bald killer or the persecuted persecutor rules over Hungary makes no difference as to the freedom of that country. I regret having to play the role of Cassandra once more and having to disappoint the fresh hopes of certain ever hopeful colleagues, but there is no possible evolution in a totalitarian society. Terror does not evolve except toward a worse terror, the scaffold does not become any more liberal, the gallows are not tolerant. Nowhere in the world has there been a party or a man with absolute power who did not use it absolutely.

The first thing to define totalitarian society, whether of the Right or of the Left, is the single party, and the single party has no reason to destroy itself. This is why the only society capable of evolution and liberalization, the only one that deserves both our critical and our active support is the society that involves a plurality of parties as a part of its structure. It alone allows one to denounce, hence to correct, injustice and crime. It alone today allows one to denounce torture, disgraceful torture, as contemptible in Algiers as in Budapest.

What Budapest was Defending

The idea, still voiced among us, that a party, because it calls itself proletarian, can enjoy special privileges in re-

gard to history is an idea of intellectuals tired of their advantages and of their freedom. History does not confer
privileges: it lets them be snatched away.

And it is not the function of intellectuals or of workers
to glorify even slightly the right of the stronger and the
fait accompli. The truth is that no one, neither individual nor party, has a right to absolute power or to lasting
privileges in a history that is itself changing. And no
privilege, no supreme reason can justify torture or terror.

On this point Budapest again showed us the way.
Hungary conquered and in chains (which our false realists compare with commiseration to Poland), still on the
edge of equilibrium, has done more for freedom and justice than any people in twenty years. But, for that lesson
to reach and convince those in the West who close their
eyes and ears, the Hungarian people (and we shall
never be consoled for this) had to shed their own blood,
and it is already drying up in people's memories.

At least we shall try to be faithful to Hungary as we
have been to Spain. In Europe's present solitude, we
have but one way of being so—which is never to betray,
at home or abroad, that for which the Hungarian combatants died and never to justify even indirectly, at home or
abroad, what killed them.

The untiring insistence upon freedom and truth, the
community of the worker and the intellectual (who are
still stupidly warring here, as tyranny aims to keep them
doing), and, finally, political democracy as a necessary
and indispensable (though surely not sufficient) condition of economic democracy—this is what Budapest was
defending. And in doing so, the great city in insurrec-

tion reminded Western Europe of its forgotten truth and greatness. It made short work of that odd feeling of inferiority that debilitates most of our intellectuals but that I, for one, refuse to feel.

Reply to Shepilov

The defects of the West are innumerable, its crimes and errors very real. But in the end, let's not forget that we are the only ones to have the possibility of improvement and emancipation that lies in free genius. Let's not forget that when totalitarian society, by its very principles, forces the friend to denounce his friend, Western society, despite its wanderings from the path of virtue, always produces a race of men who uphold honor in life—I mean men who stretch out their hands even to their enemy to save him from suffering or death.

When Minister Shepilov on his return from Paris dares to write that "Western art is bound to tear the human soul apart and to form butchers of every sort," it is time to reply to him that at least our writers and artists have never butchered anyone and that yet they are generous enough not to blame the theory of socialist realism for the massacres ordered by Shepilov and those who resemble him.

The truth is that there is room for everything among us, even for evil, and even for Shepilov's writers. There is room also for honor, for the freedom to desire, for the adventure of the mind. Whereas there is room for nothing in Stalinist culture except for edifying sermons, colorless life, and the catechism of propaganda. To any who still had any doubts about this, the Hungarian writers have just shouted the truth before choosing permanent silence today when they are ordered to lie.

It will be hard for us to be worthy of so many sacrifices. But we must try to do so in a Europe at last united, by forgetting our quarrels, by getting rid of our own errors, by multiplying our creations and our solidarity. And to those who wanted to humble us and persuade us that history could justify a reign of terror, we shall reply by our real faith that we share, as we now know, with Hungarian writers, Polish writers, and even, indeed, with Russian writers, who are also gagged.

Our faith is that throughout the world, beside the impulse toward coercion and death that is darkening history, there is a growing impulse toward persuasion and life, a vast emancipatory movement called culture that is made up both of free creation and of free work.

Our daily task, our long vocation is to add to that culture by our labors and not to subtract, even temporarily, anything from it. But our proudest duty is to defend personally to the very end, against the impulse toward coercion and death, the freedom of that culture—in other words, the freedom of work and of creation.

The Hungarian workers and intellectuals, beside whom we stand today with so much impotent grief, realized that and made us realize it. This is why, if their suffering is ours, their hope belongs to us too. Despite their destitution, their exile, their chains, it took them but a single day to transmit to us the royal legacy of liberty. May we be worthy of it!

FRANC-TIREUR, *18 March 1957*

SOCIALISM OF THE GALLOWS

(INTERVIEW)

1) Do you think that it is still possible to link the cause of truth with a Party, a State, or any organization whatever and to have complete confidence in it as if it could not possibly fail in its mission? Do you think it is still possible, in good faith, to speak of a "camp of peace"? Don't you think rather that such an attitude stands now for the most serious form of "alienation" of conscience?

IF ABSOLUTE truth belongs to anyone in this world, it certainly does not belong to the man or party that claims to possess it. When historical truth is involved, the more anyone claims to possess it the more he lies. In the final analysis, he becomes the murderer of truth. The Hungarian uprising was originally directed against a generalized lie. Hence it was necessary to assassinate the men who were fighting the lie and then try to dishonor them through a reversed lie by calling them Fascists.

As for the "camp of peace," it is better to ask the question of the former "partisans of peace" who mobilized at the time of the Stockholm appeal to outlaw atomic weapons and who now have to reconcile this with Bulganin's ultimatum threatening England, France, and incidentally Israel, with atomic rockets. It is better to ask them the question, because apparently they are not asking it of themselves.

The truth is that no nation has a monopoly on peace. Not even, as we now know, the "neutral" nations of the Orient. The way in which they—the Arab countries (except Tunisia),[1] and especially India (yes, the India of Gandhi)—betrayed Hungary and their own principles puts them henceforth on the same footing with the other nations. The nations of the Bandung group could have helped save a great European nation from slavery and death. This would have amounted to admitting and partially rewarding the efforts of all free Europeans who freely argued the cause of the colonized peoples. But the Bandung group rapidly became realistic. Apparently it is easy to become an adult in history. Consequently, those new nations must henceforth be judged as adults, on the basis of their deeds, without any special indulgence. And their attitude toward the Hungarian massacre is inexcusable. Most likely the future will show that such a self-centered sidestepping of the issue will not

[1] As for Algeria, so far as I know only the M.N.A. of Messali Hadj protested the Soviet intervention in Hungary without relinquishing any of its own protests. I was not aware of any protest on the part of the F.L.N.

pay off. The moral advantage those nations derived from the fact that they had been oppressed in the recent past was wasted by them in a few days.

Hence we shall say that some nations are merely more bellicose than others. It seems, if I can believe the progressive newspapers (which previously thought or said the opposite), that America has been less bellicose than Russia of late. But there is no need for anyone to show us that socialism can, quite as well as capitalism, foment wars. All it takes is a little will to power, and there is scarcely any nation without that (except for those which have no army, and even then you can't be sure). This wasn't known before simply because there was no socialist state. Now we know. Alienation is in any case too noble a word to describe the attitude of those who insist on seeing nothing but doves in the East and vultures in the West. Blindness, frenzy of the slave, or nihilistic admiration of force seems to me a more exact term.

Truth Is Relative

2) Do you think that, despite the situation, we can continue to attribute more weight to considerations of political expediency than to the impulse that makes us see the factual truth first of all? In this case what in your opinion is the criterion of such expediency?

Expediencies must be examined to see the dose of truth
they contain, the lesson to be drawn from them in order
to correct what had previously been thought right. But
they cannot be given an advantage over the pursuit of
factual truths. Above all, we cannot grant expediency
any precedence over regard for truth, as the Communists do and the Leftist intellectuals who follow them,
for such systematic relativism leads to the death of intelligence and the oppression of the worker. A press or a
book is not true because it is revolutionary. It has a
chance of being revolutionary only if it tries to tell the
truth. We have a right to think that truth with a capital
letter is relative. But facts are facts. And whoever says
that the sky is blue when it is gray is prostituting words
and preparing the way for tyranny.

Expediency for a Communist newspaper perhaps
amounts to saying that the whole population of Hungary is fascist except Kadar, his policemen, and his executioners. But the factual truth is that we have seen a
revolt of workers, intellectuals, and peasants who
wanted national independence and personal freedom.
The real fascism, to speak clearly, is the fascism of Kadar
and Khrushchev, who methodically crushed a popular
revolt, and of the Russian government, which permitted it.

I confess that I don't understand either the sense of
expediency that urged some of our militant progressives,
after they had denounced the Soviet intervention in
Hungary, to recommend in their congress a unified action with the French Communists, who continually insult the insurgents. Their recommendation came at a

time when Hungarians were still being hanged (just yesterday a girl of twenty) and at the very moment when a representative of the French Communist party declared that, under the same circumstances, he would be willing for the U.S.S.R. to inflict on France the same treatment it is giving Hungary. Such obsequiousness eventually becomes overwhelming. Can it be that the Communists and progressive militants feel such love for the Russians they have never seen? No, but they feel such a loathing for a part of the French, the part that loathed them enough to be willing to serve the cause of Hitler. If France is to disappear, rest assured that she will die poisoned by these two hatreds.

The Intellectual Must Take Sides

3) If the contrary is true, what can the intellectual do today? Does he have a duty, in each and every circumstance, to express his feeling and opinion publicly and to anyone at all? Or else, because of the seriousness of events and the lack of valid political forces, do you feel that one can do no better than to carry on one's own work as well as one can?

It is better for the intellectual not to talk all the time. To begin with, it would exhaust him, and, above all, it would keep him from thinking. He must create if he can, first and foremost, especially if his creation does not side-step the problems of his time. But in certain exceptional circumstances (Spanish war, Hitlerian persecutions and concentration camps, Stalinist trials and concentration camps, Hungarian war) he must leave no room for doubt as to the side he takes; he must be very careful not to let his choice be clouded by wily distinctions or discreet balancing tricks, and to leave no question as to his personal determination to defend liberty. Groupings of intellectuals can, in certain cases, and particularly when the liberty of the masses and of the spirit is mortally threatened, constitute a strength and exert an influence; Hungarian intellectuals have just proved this. However, it should be pointed out for our own guidance in the West that the continual signing of manifestoes and protests is one of the surest ways of undermining the efficacy and dignity of the intellectual. There exists a permanent blackmail that we all know and that we must have the often solitary courage to resist.

Conformity Is on the Left

Subject to these reservations, we must hope for a common rallying. But first our Leftist intellectuals, who have swallowed so many insults and may well have to begin doing so again, would have to undertake a critique of the reasonings and ideologies to which they have hitherto subscribed, which have wreaked the havoc they have seen in our most recent history. That will be the hardest thing. We must admit that today conformity is on the Left. To be sure, the Right is not brilliant. But the Left is in complete decadence, a prisoner of words, caught in its own vocabulary, capable merely of stereotyped replies, constantly at a loss when faced with the truth, from which it nevertheless claimed to derive its laws. The Left is schizophrenic and needs doctoring through pitiless self-criticism, exercise of the heart, close reasoning, and a little modesty. Until such an effort at re-examination is well under way, any rallying will be useless and even harmful. Meanwhile, the intellectual's role will be to say that the king is naked when he is, and not to go into raptures over his imaginary trappings.

In order to strike a constructive note, however, I shall propose as one of the preliminaries to any future gathering the unqualified acceptance of the following principle: none of the evils that totalitarianism (defined by the single party and the suppression of all opposition) claims to remedy is worse than totalitariansim itself.

In conclusion, I believe (as people say: I believe in God, creator of heaven and earth) that the indispensable conditions for intellectual creation and historical justice are liberty and the free confronting of differences. Without freedom, no art; art lives only on the restraints it imposes on itself, and dies of all others. But without freedom, no socialism either, except the socialism of the gallows.

DEMAIN, 21–27 *February 1957*

REFLECTIONS
ON THE GUILLOTINE

(From the book *Réflexions sur la
peine Capitale,* a symposium by Ar-
thur Koestler and Albert Camus,
published by Calmann-Lévy in 1957)

SHORTLY before the war of 1914, an assassin
whose crime was particularly repulsive (he had
slaughtered a family of farmers, including the children)
was condemned to death in Algiers. He was a farm
worker who had killed in a sort of bloodthirsty frenzy
but had aggravated his case by robbing his victims. The
affair created a great stir. It was generally thought that
decapitation was too mild a punishment for such a monster. This was the opinion, I have been told, of my father, who was especially aroused by the murder of the
children. One of the few things I know about him, in
any case, is that he wanted to witness the execution, for
the first time in his life. He got up in the dark to go to
the place of execution at the other end of town amid a
great crowd of people. What he saw that morning he
never told anyone. My mother relates merely that he
came rushing home, his face distorted, refused to talk,
lay down for a moment on the bed, and suddenly began
to vomit. He had just discovered the reality hidden under the noble phrases with which it was masked. Instead
of thinking of the slaughtered children, he could think
of nothing but that quivering body that had just been
dropped onto a board to have its head cut off.
    Presumably that ritual act is horrible indeed if it man-

ages to overcome the indignation of a simple, straightforward man and if a punishment he considered richly deserved had no other effect in the end than to nauseate him. When the extreme penalty simply causes vomiting on the part of the respectable citizen it is supposed to protect, how can anyone maintain that it is likely, as it ought to be, to bring more peace and order into the community? Rather, it is obviously no less repulsive than the crime, and this new murder, far from making amends for the harm done to the social body, adds a new blot to the first one. Indeed, no one dares speak directly of the ceremony. Officials and journalists who have to talk about it, as if they were aware of both its provocative and its shameful aspects, have made up a sort of ritual language, reduced to stereotyped phrases. Hence we read at breakfast time in a corner of the newspaper that the condemned "has paid his debt to society" or that he has "atoned" or that "at five a.m. justice was done." The officials call the condemned man "the interested party" or "the patient" or refer to him by a number. People write of capital punishment as if they were whispering. In our well-policed society we recognize that an illness is serious from the fact that we don't dare speak of it directly. For a long time, in middle-class families people said no more than that the elder daughter had a "suspicious cough" or that the father had a "growth" because tuberculosis and cancer were looked upon as somewhat shameful maladies. This is probably even truer of capital punishment since everyone strives to refer to it only through euphemisms. It is to the body politic what cancer is to the individual body, with this difference: no one has ever spoken of the necessity of cancer. There is no hesitation, on the other hand, about presenting capital punishment as a regrettable necessity, a necessity that justifies killing because it is necessary, and let's not talk about it because it is regrettable.

But it is my intention to talk about it crudely. Not because I like scandal, nor, I believe, because of an unhealthy streak in my nature. As a writer, I have always loathed avoiding the issue; as a man, I believe that the repulsive aspects of our condition, if they are inevitable, must merely be faced in silence. But when silence or tricks of language contribute to maintaining an abuse that must be reformed or a suffering that can be relieved, then there is no other solution but to speak out and show the obscenity hidden under the verbal cloak. France shares with England and Spain the honor of being one of the last countries this side of the iron curtain to keep capital punishment in its arsenal of repression. The survival of such a primitive rite has been made possible among us only by the thoughtlessness or ignorance of the public, which reacts only with the ceremonial phrases that have been drilled into it. When the imagination sleeps, words are emptied of their meaning: a deaf population absent-mindedly registers the condemnation of a man. But if people are shown the machine, made to touch the wood and steel and to hear the sound of a head falling, then public imagination, suddenly awakened, will repudiate both the vocabulary and the penalty.

When the Nazis in Poland indulged in public executions of hostages, to keep those hostages from shouting words of revolt and liberty they muzzled them with a plaster-coated gag. It would be shocking to compare the fate of those innocent victims with that of condemned criminals. But, aside from the fact that criminals are not the only ones to be guillotined in our country, the method is the same. We smother under padded words a penalty whose legitimacy we could assert only after we had examined the penalty in reality. Instead of saying that the death penalty is first of all necessary and then adding that it is better not to talk about it, it is essential to say what it really is and then say whether, being what it is, it is to be considered as necessary.

So far as I am concerned, I consider it not only useless but definitely harmful, and I must record my opinion here before getting to the subject itself. It would not be fair to imply that I reached this conclusion as a result of the weeks of investigation and research I have just devoted to this question. But it would be just as unfair to attribute my conviction to mere mawkishness. I am far from indulging in the flabby pity characteristic of humanitarians, in which values and responsibilities fuse, crimes are balanced against one another, and innocence finally loses its rights. Unlike many of my well-known contemporaries, I do not think that man is by nature a social animal. To tell the truth, I think just the reverse. But I believe, and this is quite different, that he cannot live henceforth outside of society, whose laws are necessary to his physical survival. Hence the responsibilities must be established by society itself according to a reasonable and workable scale. But the law's final justification is in the good it does or fails to do to the society of a given place and time. For years I have been unable to see anything in capital punishment but a penalty the imagination could not endure and a lazy disorder that my reason condemned. Yet I was ready to think that my imagination was influencing my judgment. But, to tell the truth, I found during my recent research nothing that did not strengthen my conviction, nothing that modified my arguments. On the contrary, to the arguments I already had others were added. Today I share absolutely Koestler's conviction: the death penalty besmirches our society, and its upholders cannot reasonably defend it. Without repeating his decisive defense, without piling up facts and figures that would only duplicate others (and Jean Bloch-Michel's make them useless), I shall merely state reasons to be added to Koestler's; like his, they argue for an immediate abolition of the death penalty.

We all know that the great argument of those who defend capital punishment is the exemplary value of the punishment. Heads are cut off not only to punish but to intimidate, by a frightening example, any who might be tempted to imitate the guilty. Society is not taking revenge; it merely wants to forestall. It waves the head in the air so that potential murderers will see their fate and recoil from it.

This argument would be impressive if we were not obliged to note:

1) that society itself does not believe in the exemplary value it talks about;

2) that there is no proof that the death penalty ever made a single murderer recoil when he had made up his mind, whereas clearly it had no effect but one of fascination on thousands of criminals;

3) that, in other regards, it constitutes a repulsive example, the consequences of which cannot be foreseen.

To begin with, society does not believe in what it says. If it really believed what it says, it would exhibit the heads. Society would give executions the benefit of the publicity it generally uses for national bond issues or new brands of drinks. But we know that executions in our country, instead of taking place publicly, are now perpetrated in prison courtyards before a limited number of specialists. We are less likely to know why and since when. This is a relatively recent measure. The last public execution, which took place in 1939, beheaded Weidmann, the author of several murders, who was notorious for his crimes. That morning a large crowd gathered at Versailles, including a large number of photographers. Between the moment when Weidmann was shown to the crowd and the moment when he was decapitated, photographs could be taken. A few hours later *Paris-Soir* published a page of illustrations of that appetizing event. Thus the good people of Paris could see that the light precision instrument used by the executioner was as different from the historical scaffold as a Jaguar is from one of our old Pierce-Arrows. The administration and the government, contrary to all hope, took such excellent publicity very badly and protested that the press had tried to satisfy the sadistic instincts of its readers. Consequently, it was decided that executions would no longer take place publicly, an arrangement that, soon after, facilitated the work of the occupation authorities. Logic, in that affair, was not on the side of the lawmaker.

On the contrary, a special decoration should have been awarded to the editor of *Paris-Soir*, thereby encouraging him to do better the next time. If the penalty is intended to be exemplary, then, not only should the photographs be multiplied, but the machine should even be set on a platform in Place de la Concorde at two p.m., the entire population should be invited, and the ceremony should be put on television for those who couldn't attend. Either this must be done or else there must be no more talk of exemplary value. How can a furtive assassination committed at night in a prison courtyard be exemplary? At most, it serves the purpose of periodically informing the citizens that they will die if they happen to kill—a future that can be promised even to those who do not kill. For the penalty to be truly exemplary it must be frightening. Tuaut de La Bouverie, representative of the people in 1791 and a partisan of public executions, was more logical when he declared to the National Assembly: "It takes a terrifying spectacle to hold the people in check."

Today there is no spectacle, but only a penalty known to all by hearsay and, from time to time, the news of an execution dressed up in soothing phrases. How could a future criminal keep in mind, at the moment of his crime, a sanction that everyone strives to make more and more abstract? And if it is really desired that he constantly keep that sanction in mind so that it will first balance and later reverse a frenzied decision, should there not be an effort to engrave that sanction and its dreadful reality in the sensitivity of all by every visual and verbal means?

Instead of vaguely evoking a debt that someone this very morning paid society, would it not be a more effective example to remind each taxpayer in detail of what he may expect? Instead of saying: "If you kill, you will atone for it on the scaffold," wouldn't it be better to tell him, for purposes of example: "If you kill, you will be imprisoned for months or years, torn between an impossible despair and a constantly renewed terror, until one morning we shall slip into your cell after removing our shoes the better to take you by surprise while you are sound asleep after the night's anguish. We shall fall on you, tie your hands behind your back, cut with scissors your shirt collar and your hair if need be. Perfectionists that we are, we shall bind your arms with a strap so that you are forced to stoop and your neck will be more accessible. Then we shall carry you, an assistant on each side supporting you by the arm, with your feet dragging behind through the corridors. Then, under a night sky, one of the executioners will finally seize you by the seat of your pants and throw you horizontally on a board while another will steady your head in the lunette and a third will let fall from a height of seven feet a hundred-and-twenty-pound blade that will slice off your head like a razor."

For the example to be even better, for the terror to impress each of us sufficiently to outweigh at the right moment an irresistible desire for murder, it would be essential to go still further. Instead of boasting, with the pretentious thoughtlessness characteristic of us, of having invented this rapid and humane [1] method of killing condemned men, we should publish thousands of copies of the eyewitness accounts and medical reports describing the state of the body after the execution, to be read in schools and universities. Particularly suitable for this purpose is the recent report to the Academy of Medicine made by Doctors Piedelièvre and Fournier. Those courageous doctors, invited in the interest of science to examine the bodies of the guillotined after the execution, considered it their duty to sum up their dreadful observations: "If we may be permitted to give our opinion, such sights are frightfully painful. The blood flows from the blood vessels at the speed of the severed carotids, then it coagulates. The muscles contract and their fibrillation is stupefying; the intestines ripple and the heart moves irregularly, incompletely, fascinatingly. The mouth puckers at certain moments in a terrible pout. It is true that in that severed head the eyes are motionless with dilated pupils; fortunately they look at nothing and, if they are devoid of the cloudiness and opalescence of the corpse, they have no motion; their transparence belongs to life, but their fixity belongs to death. All this can last minutes, even hours, in sound specimens: death is not immediate. . . . Thus, every vital element survives decapitation. The doctor is left with this impression of a horrible experience, of a murderous vivisection, followed by a premature burial." [2]

---

[1] According to the optimistic Dr. Guillotin, the condemned was not to feel anything. At most a "slight sensation of coldness on his neck."

[2] *Justice sans bourreau*, No. 2 (June 1956).

I doubt that there are many readers who can read that terrifying report without blanching. Consequently, its exemplary power and its capacity to intimidate can be counted on. There is no reason not to add to it eyewitness accounts that confirm the doctors' observations. Charlotte Corday's severed head blushed, it is said, under the executioner's slap. This will not shock anyone who listens to more recent observers. An executioner's assistant (hence hardly suspect of indulging in romanticizing and sentimentality) describes in these terms what he was forced to see: "It was a madman undergoing a real attack of *delirium tremens* that we dropped under the blade. The head dies at once. But the body literally jumps about in the basket, straining on the cords. Twenty minutes later, at the cemetery, it is still quivering." [3] The present chaplain of the Santé prison, Father Devoyod (who does not seem opposed to capital punishment), gives in his book, *Les Délinquants*,[4] an account that goes rather far and renews the story of Languille, whose decapitated head answered the call of his name:[5] "The morning of the execution, the condemned man was in a very bad mood and refused the consolations of religion. Knowing his heart of hearts and the affection he had for his wife, who was very devout, we said to him: 'Come now, out of love for your wife, commune with yourself a moment before dying,' and the condemned man accepted. He communed at length before the crucifix, then he seemed to pay no further attention to our

[3] Published by Roger Grenier in *Les Monstres* (Gallimard). These declarations are authentic.

[4] Editions Matot-Braine, Reims.   [5] In 1905 in the Loiret.

presence. When he was executed, we were a short distance from him. His head fell into the trough in front of the guillotine and the body was immediately put into the basket; but, by some mistake, the basket was closed before the head was put in. The assistant who was carrying the head had to wait a moment until the basket was opened again; now, during that brief space of time we could see the condemned man's eyes fixed on me with a look of supplication, as if to ask forgiveness. Instinctively we made the sign of the cross to bless the head, and then the lids blinked, the expression of the eyes softened, and finally the look, that had remained full of expression, became vague. . . ." The reader may or may not, according to his faith, accept the explanation provided by the priest. At least those eyes that "had remained full of expression" need no interpretation.

I could adduce other first-hand accounts that would be just as hallucinating. But I, for one, could not go on. After all, I do not claim that capital punishment is exemplary, and the penalty seems to me just what it is, a crude surgery practiced under conditions that leave nothing edifying about it. Society, on the other hand, and the State, which is not so impressionable, can very well put up with such details and, since they extol an example, ought to try to get everyone to put up with them so that no one will be ignorant of them and the population, terrorized once and for all, will become Franciscan one and all. Whom do they hope to intimidate, otherwise, by that example forever hidden, by the threat of a punishment described as easy and swift and easier to bear, after all, than cancer, by a penalty submerged in the flowers of rhetoric? Certainly not those who are considered respectable (some of them are) because they are sleeping at that hour, and the great example has not been announced to them, and they will be eating their toast and marmalade at the time of the premature burial, and they will be informed of the work of justice, if perchance they read the newspapers, by an insipid news item that will melt like sugar in their memory. And, yet, those peaceful creatures are the ones who provide the largest percentage of homicides. Many such respectable people are potential criminals. According to a magistrate, the vast majority of murderers he had known did not know when shaving in the morning that they were going to kill later in the day. As an example and for the sake of security, it would be wiser, instead of hiding the execution, to hold up the severed head in front of all who are shaving in the morning.

Nothing of the sort happens. The State disguises executions and keeps silent about these statements and eyewitness accounts. Hence it doesn't believe in the exemplary value of the penalty, except by tradition and because it has never bothered to think about the matter. The criminal is killed because this has been done for centuries and, besides, he is killed in a way that was set at the end of the eighteenth century. Out of habit, people will turn to arguments that were used centuries ago, even though these arguments must be contradicted by measures that the evolution of public sensitivity has made inevitable. A law is applied without being thought out and the condemned die in the name of a theory in which the executioners do not believe. If they believed in it, this would be obvious to all. But publicity not only arouses sadistic instincts with incalculable repercussions eventually leading to another murder; it also runs the risk of provoking revolt and disgust in the public opinion. It would become harder to execute men one after another, as is done in our country today, if those executions were translated into vivid images in the popular imagination. The man who enjoys his coffee while reading that justice has been done would spit it out at the least detail. And the texts I have quoted might seem to vindicate certain professors of criminal law who, in their obvious inability to justify that anachronistic penalty, console themselves by declaring, with the sociologist Tarde, that it is better to cause death without causing suffering than it is to cause suffering without causing death. This is why we must approve the position of Gambetta, who, as an adversary of the death penalty, voted against a bill involving suppression of publicity for executions, declaring: "If you suppress the horror of the spectacle, if you execute inside prisons, you will smother the public outburst of revolt that has taken place of late and you will strengthen the death penalty."

Indeed, one must kill publicly or confess that one does not feel authorized to kill. If society justifies the death penalty by the necessity of the example, it must justify itself by making the publicity necessary. It must show the executioner's hands each time and force everyone to look at them—the over-delicate citizens and all those who had any responsibility in bringing the executioner into being. Otherwise, society admits that it kills without knowing what it is saying or doing. Or else it admits that such revolting ceremonies can only excite crime or completely upset opinion. Who could better state this than a magistrate at the end of his career, Judge Falco, whose brave confession deserves serious reflection: "The only time in my life when I decided against a commutation of penalty and in favor of execution, I thought that, despite my position, I could attend the execution and remain utterly impassive. Moreover, the criminal was not very interesting: he had tormented his daughter and finally thrown her into a well. But, after his execution, for weeks and even months, my nights were haunted by that recollection. . . . Like everyone else, I served in the war and saw an innocent generation die, but I can state that nothing gave me the sort of bad conscience I felt in the face of the kind of administrative murder that is called capital punishment." [6]

But, after all, why should society believe in that example when it does not stop crime, when its effects, if they exist, are invisible? To begin with, capital punishment could not intimidate the man who doesn't know that he is going to kill, who makes up his mind to it in a flash and commits his crime in a state of frenzy or obsession, nor the man who, going to an appointment to have it out with someone, takes along a weapon to frighten the faithless one or the opponent and uses it although he didn't want to or didn't think he wanted to. In other words, it could not intimidate the man who is hurled into crime as if into a calamity. This is tantamount to saying that it is powerless in the majority of cases. It is only fair to point out that in our country capital punishment

[6] *Réalités*, No. 105 (October 1954).

is rarely applied in such cases. But the word "rarely" it-self makes one shudder.

Does it frighten at least that race of criminals on whom it claims to operate and who live off crime? Nothing is less certain. We can read in Koestler that at a time when pickpockets were executed in England, other pickpock-ets exercised their talents in the crowd surrounding the scaffold where their colleague was being hanged. Statis-tics drawn up at the beginning of the century in England show that out of 250 who were hanged, 170 had previ-ously attended one or more executions. And in 1886, out of 167 condemned men who had gone through the Bristol prison, 164 had witnessed at least one execution. Such statistics are no longer possible to gather in France because of the secrecy surrounding executions. But they give cause to think that around my father, the day of that execution, there must have been a rather large number of future criminals, who did not vomit. The power of intimidation reaches only the quiet individuals who are not drawn toward crime and has no effect on the hard-ened ones who need to be softened. In Koestler's essay and in the detailed studies will be found the most con-vincing facts and figures on this aspect of the subject.

It cannot be denied, however, that men fear death. The privation of life is indeed the supreme penalty and ought to excite in them a decisive fear. The fear of death, arising from the most obscure depths of the individual, ravages him; the instinct to live, when it is threatened, panics and struggles in agony. Therefore the legislator was right in thinking that his law was based upon one of the most mysterious and most powerful incentives of human nature. But law is always simpler than nature. When law ventures, in the hope of dominating, into the dark regions of consciousness, it has little chance of being able to simplify the complexity it wants to codify.

If fear of death is, indeed, a fact, another fact is that such fear, however great it may be, has never sufficed to quell human passions. Bacon is right in saying that there is no passion so weak that it cannot confront and overpower fear of death. Revenge, love, honor, pain, another fear manage to overcome it. How could cupidity, hatred, jealousy fail to do what love of a person or a country, what a passion for freedom manage to do? For centuries the death penalty, often accompanied by barbarous refinements, has been trying to hold crime in check; yet crime persists. Why? Because the instincts that are warring in man are not, as the law claims, constant forces in a state of equilibrium. They are variable forces constantly waxing and waning, and their repeated lapses from equilibrium nourish the life of the mind as electrical oscillations, when close enough, set up a current. Just imagine the series of oscillations, from desire to lack of appetite, from decision to renunciation, through which each of us passes in a single day, multiply these variations infinitely, and you will have an idea of psychological proliferation. Such lapses from equilibrium are generally too fleeting to allow a single force to dominate the whole being. But it may happen that one of the soul's forces breaks loose until it fills the whole field of consciousness; at such a moment no instinct, not even that of life, can oppose the tyranny of that irresistible force. For capital punishment to be really intimidating, human nature would have to be different; it would have to be as stable and serene as the law itself. But then human nature would be dead.

It is not dead. This is why, however surprising this may seem to anyone who has never observed or directly experienced human complexity, the murderer, most of the time, feels innocent when he kills. Every criminal acquits himself before he is judged. He considers himself, if not within his right, at least excused by circumstances. He does not think or foresee; when he thinks, it is to foresee that he will be forgiven altogether or in part. How could he fear what he considers highly improbable? He will fear death after the verdict but not before the crime. Hence the law, to be intimidating, should leave the murderer no chance, should be implacable in advance and particularly admit no extenuating circumstance. But who among us would dare ask this?

If anyone did, it would still be necessary to take into account another paradox of human nature. If the instinct to live is fundamental, it is no more so than another instinct of which the academic psychologists do not speak: the death instinct, which at certain moments calls for the destruction of oneself and of others. It is probable that the desire to kill often coincides with the desire to die or to annihilate oneself.[7] Thus, the instinct for self-preservation is matched, in variable proportions, by the instinct for destruction. The latter is the only way of explaining altogether the various perversions which,

[7] It is possible to read every week in the papers of criminals who originally hesitated between killing themselves and killing others.

from alcoholism to drugs, lead an individual to his death while he knows full well what is happening. Man wants to live, but it is useless to hope that this desire will dictate all his actions. He also wants to be nothing; he wants the irreparable, and death for its own sake. So it happens that the criminal wants not only the crime but the suffering that goes with it, even (one might say, especially) if that suffering is exceptional. When that odd desire grows and becomes dominant, the prospect of being put to death not only fails to stop the criminal, but probably even adds to the vertigo in which he swoons. Thus, in a way, he kills in order to die.

Such peculiarities suffice to explain why a penalty that seems calculated to frighten normal minds is in reality altogether unrelated to ordinary psychology. All statistics without exception, those concerning countries that have abolished execution as well as the others, show that there is no connection between the abolition of the death penalty and criminality.[8] Criminal statistics neither increase nor decrease. The guillotine exists, and so does crime; between the two there is no other apparent connection than that of the law. All we can conclude from the figures, set down at length in statistical tables, is this: for centuries crimes other than murder were punished with death, and the supreme punishment, repeated over and over again, did not do away with any

[8] Report of the English Select Committee of 1930 and of the English Royal Commission that recently resumed the study: "All the statistics we have examined confirm the fact that abolition of the death penalty has not provoked an increase in the number of crimes."

of those crimes. For centuries now, those crimes have no longer been punished with death. Yet they have not increased; in fact, some of them have decreased. Similarly, murder has been punished with execution for centuries and yet the race of Cain has not disappeared. Finally, in the thirty-three nations that have abolished the death penalty or no longer use it, the number of murders has not increased. Who could deduce from this that capital punishment is really intimidating?

Conservatives cannot deny these facts or these figures. Their only and final reply is significant. They explain the paradoxical attitude of a society that so carefully hides the executions it claims to be exemplary. "Nothing proves, indeed," say the conservatives, "that the death penalty is exemplary; as a matter of fact, it is certain that thousands of murderers have not been intimidated by it. But there is no way of knowing those it has intimidated; consequently, nothing proves that it is not exemplary." Thus, the greatest of punishments, the one that involves the last dishonor for the condemned and grants the supreme privilege to society, rests on nothing but an unverifiable possibility. Death, on the other hand, does not involve degrees or probabilities. It solidifies all things, culpability and the body, in a definitive rigidity. Yet it is administered among us in the name of chance and a calculation. Even if that calculation were reasonable, should there not be a certainty to authorize the most certain of deaths? However, the condemned is cut in two, not so much for the crime he committed but by virtue of all the crimes that might have been and were not committed, that can be and will not be committed. The most sweeping uncertainty in this case authorizes the most implacable certainty.

I am not the only one to be amazed by such a dangerous contradiction. Even the State condemns it, and such bad conscience explains in turn the contradiction of its own attitude. The State divests its executions of all publicity because it cannot assert, in the face of facts, that they ever served to intimidate criminals. The State cannot escape the dilemma Beccaria described when he wrote: "If it is important to give the people proofs of power often, then executions must be frequent; but crimes will have to be frequent too, and this will prove that the death penalty does not make the complete impression that it should, whence it results that it is both useless and necessary." What can the State do with a penalty that is useless and necessary, except to hide it without abolishing it? The State will keep it then, a little out of the way, not without embarrassment, in the blind hope that one man at least, one day at least, will be stopped from his murderous gesture by thought of the punishment and, without anyone's ever knowing it, will justify a law that has neither reason nor experience in its favor. In order to continue claiming that the guillotine is exemplary, the State is consequently led to multiply very real murders in the hope of avoiding a possible murder which, as far as it knows or ever will know, may never be perpetrated. An odd law, to be sure, which knows the murder it commits and will never know the one it prevents.

What will be left of that power of example if it is proved that capital punishment has another power, and a very real one, which degrades men to the point of shame, madness, and murder?

It is already possible to follow the exemplary effects of such ceremonies on public opinion, the manifestations of sadism they arouse, the hideous vainglory they excite in certain criminals. No nobility in the vicinity of the gallows, but disgust, contempt, or the vilest indulgence of the senses. These effects are well known. Decency forced the guillotine to emigrate from Place de l'Hotel de Ville to the city gates, then into the prisons. We are less informed as to the feelings of those whose job it is to attend such spectacles. Just listen then to the warden of an English prison who confesses to "a keen sense of personal shame" and to the chaplain who speaks of "horror, shame, and humiliation." [9] Just imagine the feelings of the man who kills under orders—I mean the executioner. What can we think of those officials who call the guillotine "the shunting engine," the condemned man "the client" or "the parcel"? The priest Bela Just, who accompanied more than thirty condemned men, writes: "The slang of the administrators of justice is quite as cynical and vulgar as that of the criminals." [1] And here are the remarks of one of our assistant executioners on his journeys to the provinces: "When we would start on a trip, it was always a lark, with taxis and the best restaurants part of the spree!" [2] The same one says, boasting of the executioner's skill

[9] Report of the Select Committee, 1930.
[1] *La Potence et la Croix* (Fasquelle).
[2] Roger Grenier: *Les Monstres* (Gallimard).

in releasing the blade: "You could *allow yourself the fun* of pulling the client's hair." The dissoluteness expressed here has other, deeper aspects. The clothing of the condemned belongs in principle to the executioner. The elder Deibler used to hang all such articles of clothing in a shed and *now and then would go and look at them*. But there are more serious aspects. Here is what our assistant executioner declares: "The new executioner is batty about the guillotine. He sometimes spends days on end at home sitting on a chair, ready with hat and coat on, waiting for a summons from the Ministry." [3]

Yes, this is the man of whom Joseph de Maistre said that, for him to exist, there had to be a special decree from the divine power and that, without him, "order yields to chaos, thrones collapse, and society disappears." This is the man through whom society rids itself altogether of the guilty man, for the executioner signs the prison release and takes charge of a free man. The fine and solemn example, thought up by our legislators, at least produces one sure effect—to depreciate or to destroy all humanity and reason in those who take part in it directly. But, it will be said, these are exceptional creatures who find a vocation in such dishonor. They seem less exceptional when we learn that hundreds of persons offer to serve as executioners without pay. The men of our generation, who have lived through the history of recent years, will not be astonished by this bit of information. They know that behind the most peaceful and familiar faces slumbers the impulse to torture and

[3] Ibid.

murder. The punishment that aims to intimidate an unknown murderer certainly confers a vocation of killer
on many another monster about whom there is no doubt.
And since we are busy justifying our cruelest laws with
probable considerations, let there be no doubt that out
of those hundreds of men whose services were declined,
one at least must have satisfied otherwise the bloodthirsty
instincts the guillotine excited in him.

If, therefore, there is a desire to maintain the death
penalty, let us at least be spared the hypocrisy of a justification by example. Let us be frank about that penalty
which can have no publicity, that intimidation which
works only on respectable people, so long as they are respectable, which fascinates those who have ceased to
be respectable and debases or deranges those who take
part in it. It is a penalty, to be sure, a frightful torture,
both physical and moral, but it provides no sure example
except a demoralizing one. It punishes, but it forestalls
nothing; indeed, it may even arouse the impulse to murder. It hardly seems to exist, except for the man who
suffers it—in his soul for months and years, in his body
during the desperate and violent hour when he is cut
in two without suppressing his life. Let us call it by the
name which, for lack of any other nobility, will at least
give the nobility of truth, and let us recognize it for
what it is essentially: a revenge.

A punishment that penalizes without forestalling is indeed called revenge. It is a quasi-arithmetical reply
made by society to whoever breaks its primordial law.
That reply is as old as man; it is called the law of retalia-

tion. Whoever has done me harm must suffer harm; whoever has put out my eye must lose an eye; and whoever has killed must die. This is an emotion, and a particularly violent one, not a principle. Retaliation is related to nature and instinct, not to law. Law, by definition, cannot obey the same rules as nature. If murder is in the nature of man, the law is not intended to imitate or reproduce that nature. It is intended to correct it. Now, retaliation does no more than ratify and confer the status of a law on a pure impulse of nature. We have all known that impulse, often to our shame, and we know its power, for it comes down to us from the primitive forests. In this regard, we French, who are properly indignant upon seeing the oil king in Saudi Arabia preach international democracy and call in a butcher to cut off a thief's hand with a cleaver, live also in a sort of Middle Ages without even the consolations of faith. We still define justice according to the rules of a crude arithmetic.[4] Can it be said at least that that arithmetic is exact

[4] A few years ago I asked for the reprieve of six Tunisians who had been condemned to death for the murder, in a riot, of three French policemen. The circumstances in which the murder had taken place made difficult any division of responsibilities. A note from the executive office of the President of the Republic informed me that my appeal was being considered by the appropriate organization. Unfortunately, when that note was addressed to me I had already read two weeks earlier that the sentence had been carried out. Three of the condemned men had been put to death and the three others reprieved. The reasons for reprieving some rather than the others were not convincing. But probably it was essential to carry out three executions where there had been three victims.

and that jusitce, even when elementary, even when limited to legal revenge, is safeguarded by the death penalty? The answer must be no.

Let us leave aside the fact that the law of retaliation is inapplicable and that it would seem just as excessive to punish the incendiary by setting fire to his house as it would be insufficient to punish the thief by deducting from his bank account a sum equal to his theft. Let us admit that it is just and necessary to compensate for the murder of the victim by the death of the murderer. But beheading is not simply death. It is just as different, in essence, from the privation of life as a concentration camp is from prison. It is a murder, to be sure, and one that arithmetically pays for the murder committed. But it adds to death a rule, a public premeditation known to the future victim, an organization, in short, which is in itself a source of moral sufferings more terrible than death. Hence there is no equivalence. Many laws consider a premeditated crime more serious than a crime of pure violence. But what then is capital punishment but the most premeditated of murders, to which no criminal's deed, however calculated it may be, can be compared? For there to be equivalence, the death penalty would have to punish a criminal who had warned his victim of the date at which he would inflict a horrible death on him and who, from that moment onward, had confined him at his mercy for months. Such a monster is not encountered in private life.

There, too, when our official jurists talk of putting to death without causing suffering, they don't know what they are talking about and, above all, they lack imagina-

tion. The devastating, degrading fear that is imposed on
the condemned for months or years [5] is a punishment
more terrible than death, and one that was not imposed
on the victim. Even in the fright caused by the mortal
violence being done to him, most of the time the victim
is hastened to his death without knowing what is happening to him. The period of horror is counted out with
his life, and hope of escaping the madness that has swept
down upon that life probably never leaves him. On the
other hand, the horror is parceled out to the man who is
condemned to death. Torture through hope alternates
with the pangs of animal despair. The lawyer and chaplain, out of mere humanity, and the jailers, so that the
condemned man will keep quiet, are unanimous in assuring him that he will be reprieved. He believes this
with all his being and then he ceases to believe it. He
hopes by day and despairs of it by night.[6] As the weeks
pass, hope and despair increase and become equally unbearable. According to all accounts, the color of the skin

[5] Roemen, condemned to death at the Liberation of France,
remained seven hundred days in chains before being executed,
and this is scandalous. Those condemned under common law,
as a general rule, wait from three to six months for the morning
of their death. And it is difficult, if one wants to maintain
their chances of survival, to shorten that period. I can bear
witness, moreover, to the fact that the examination of appeals
for mercy is conducted in France with a seriousness that does
not exclude the visible inclination to pardon, insofar as the
law and customs permit.
[6] Sunday not being a day of execution, Saturday night is always better in the cell blocks reserved for those condemned to
death.

changes, fear acting like an acid. "Knowing that you are going to die is nothing," said a condemned man in Fresnes. "But not knowing whether or not you are going to live, that's terror and anguish." Cartouche said of the supreme punishment: "Why, it's just a few minutes that have to be lived through." But it is a matter of months, not of minutes. Long in advance the condemned man knows that he is going to be killed and that the only thing that can save him is a reprieve, rather similar, for him, to the decrees of heaven. In any case, he cannot intervene, make a plea himself, or convince. Everything goes on outside of him. He is no longer a man but a thing waiting to be handled by the executioners. He is kept as if he were inert matter, but he still has a consciousness which is his chief enemy.

When the officials whose job it is to kill that man call him a parcel, they know what they are saying. To be unable to do anything against the hand that moves you from one place to another, holds you or rejects you, is this not indeed being a parcel, or a thing, or, better, a hobbled animal? Even then an animal can refuse to eat. The condemned man cannot. He is given the benefit of a special diet (at Fresnes, Diet No. 4 with extra milk, wine, sugar, jam, butter); they see to it that he nourishes himself. If need be, he is forced to do so. The animal that is going to be killed must be in the best condition. The thing or the animal has a right only to those debased freedoms that are called whims. "They are very touchy," a top-sergeant at Fresnes says without the least irony of those condemned to death. Of course, but how else can they have contact with freedom and the dignity of the will that man cannot do without? Touchy or not, the moment the sentence has been pronounced the condemned man enters an imperturbable machine. For a certain number of weeks he travels along in the intricate machinery that determines his every gesture and eventually hands him over to those who will lay him down on the killing machine. The parcel is no longer subject to the laws of chance that hang over the living creature but to mechanical laws that allow him to foresee accurately the day of his beheading.

That day his being an object comes to an end. During the three quarters of an hour separating him from the end, the certainty of a powerless death stifles everything else; the animal, tied down and amenable, knows a hell that makes the hell he is threatened with seem ridiculous. The Greeks, after all, were more humane with their hemlock. They left their condemned a relative freedom, the possibility of putting off or hastening the hour of his death. They gave him a choice between suicide and execution. On the other hand, in order to be doubly sure, we deal with the culprit ourselves. But there could not really be any justice unless the condemned, after making known his decision months in advance, had approached his victim, bound him firmly, informed him that he would be put to death in an hour, and had finally used that hour to set up the apparatus of death. What criminal ever reduced his victim to such a desperate and powerless condition?

This doubtless explains the odd submissiveness that is customary in the condemned at the moment of their execution. These men who have nothing more to lose could play their last card, choose to die of a chance bullet or be guillotined in the kind of frantic struggle that dulls all the faculties. In a way, this would amount to dying freely. And yet, with but few exceptions, the rule is for the condemned to walk toward death passively in a sort of dreary despondency. That is probably what our journalists mean when they say that the condemned died courageously. We must read between the lines that the condemned made no noise, accepted his status as a parcel, and that everyone is grateful to him for this. In such a degrading business, the interested party shows a praiseworthy sense of propriety by keeping the degradation from lasting too long. But the compliments and the certificates of courage belong to the general mystification surrounding the death penalty. For the condemned will often be seemly in proportion to the fear he feels. He will deserve the praise of the press only if his fear or his feeling of isolation is great enough to sterilize him completely. Let there be no misunderstanding. Some among the condemned, whether political or not, die heroically, and they must be granted the proper admiration and respect. But the majority of them know only the silence of fear, only the impassivity of fright, and it seems to me that such terrified silence deserves even greater respect. When the priest Bela Just offers to write to the family of a young condemned man a few moments before he is hanged and hears the reply: "I have no courage, even for that," how can a priest, hearing that confession of weakness, fail to honor the most wretched and most sacred thing in man? Those who say nothing but leave a little pool on the spot from which they are taken—who would dare say they died as cowards? And how can we describe the men who reduced them to such cowardice? After all, every murderer when he kills runs the risk of the most dreadful of deaths, whereas those who kill him risk nothing except advancement.

No, what man experiences at such times is beyond all morality. Not virtue, nor courage, nor intelligence, nor even innocence has anything to do with it. Society is suddenly reduced to a state of primitive terrors where nothing can be judged. All equity and all dignity have disappeared. "The conviction of innocence does not immunize against brutal treatment. . . . I have seen authentic bandits die courageously whereas innocent men went to their deaths trembling in every muscle." [7] When the same man adds that, according to his experience, intellectuals show more weakness, he is not implying that such men have less courage than others but merely that they have more imagination. Having to face an inevitable death, any man, whatever his convictions, is torn asunder from head to toe.[8] The feeling of powerlessness and solitude of the condemned man, bound and up against the public coalition that demands his death, is in itself an unimaginable punishment. From this point of view, too, it would be better for the execution to be public. The actor in every man could

[7] Bela Just: op. cit.
[8] A great surgeon, a Catholic himself, told me that as a result of his experience he did not even inform believers when they had an incurable cancer. According to him, the shock might destroy even their faith.

then come to the aid of the terrified animal and help him cut a figure, even in his own eyes. But darkness and secrecy offer no recourse. In such a disaster, courage, strength of soul, even faith may be disadvantages. As a general rule, a man is undone by waiting for capital punishment well before he dies. Two deaths are inflicted on him, the first being worse than the second, whereas he killed but once. Compared to such torture, the penalty of retaliation seems like a civilized law. It never claimed that the man who gouged out one of his brother's eyes should be totally blinded.

Such a basic injustice has repercussions, besides, on the relatives of the executed man. The victim has his family, whose sufferings are generally very great and who, most often, want to be avenged. They are, but the relatives of the condemned man then discover an excess of suffering that punishes them beyond all justice. A mother's or a father's long months of waiting, the visiting-room, the artificial conversations filling up the brief moments spent with the condemned man, the visions of the execution are all tortures that were not imposed on the relatives of the victim. Whatever may be the feelings of the latter, they cannot want the revenge to extend so far beyond the crime and to torture people who share their own grief. "I have been reprieved, Father," writes a condemned man, "I can't yet realize the good fortune that has come my way. My reprieve was signed on April 30 and I was told Wednesday as I came back from the visiting-room. I immediately informed Papa and Mama, who had not yet left the prison. You can imagine their happiness." [9] We can indeed imagine it, but only insofar as we can imagine their uninterrupted suffering until the moment of the reprieve, and the final despair of those who receive the other notification, which punishes, in iniquity, their innocence and their misfortune.

To cut short this question of the law of retaliation, we must note that even in its primitive form it can operate only between two individuals of whom one is absolutely innocent and the other absolutely guilty. The victim, to be sure, is innocent. But can the society that is supposed to represent the victim lay claim to innocence? Is it not responsible, at least in part, for the crime it punishes so severely? This theme has often been developed, and I shall not repeat the arguments that all sorts of thinkers have brought forth since the eighteenth century. They can be summed up anyway by saying that every society has the criminals it deserves. But insofar as France is concerned, it is impossible not to point out the circumstances that ought to make our legislators more modest. Answering an inquiry of the *Figaro* in 1952 on the death penalty, a colonel asserted that establishing hard labor for life as the most severe penalty would amount to setting up schools of crime. That high-ranking officer seemed to be ignorant, and I can only congratulate him, of the fact that we already have our schools of crime, which differ from our federal prisons in this notable regard: it is possible to leave them at any hour of the day or

[9] Father Devoyod: op. cit. Equally impossible to read calmly the petitions for reprieve presented by a father or a mother who obviously does not understand such sudden misfortune.

night; they are the taverns and slums, the glory of our Republic. On this point it is impossible to express one-self moderately.

Statistics show 64,000 overcrowded dwellings (from three to five persons per room) in the city of Paris alone. To be sure, the killer of children is a particularly vile creature who scarcely arouses pity. It is probable, too (I say probable), that none of my readers, forced to live in the same conditions, would go so far as to kill children. Hence there is no question of reducing the culpability of certain monsters. But those monsters, in decent dwellings, would perhaps have had no occasion to go so far. The least that can be said is that they are not alone guilty, and it seems strange that the right to punish them should be granted to the very people who subsidize, not housing, but the growing of beets for the production of alcohol.[1]

But alcohol makes this scandal even more shocking. It is known that the French nation is systematically intoxicated by its parliamentary majority, for generally vile reasons. Now, the proportion of alcohol's responsibility in the cause of bloodthirsty crimes is shocking. A lawyer (Maître Guillon) estimated it at 60 per cent. For Dr. Lagriffe the proportion extends from 41.7 to 72 per cent. An investigation carried out in 1951 in the clearing-center of the Fresnes prison, among the common-law criminals, showed 29 per cent to be chronic alcoholics and 24 per cent to have an alcoholic inheritance. Finally, 95 per cent of the killers of children are alcoholics. These

[1] France ranks first among countries for its consumption of alcohol and fifteenth in building.

are impressive figures. We can balance them with an even more magnificent figure: the tax report of a firm producing *apéritifs,* which in 1953 showed a profit of 410 million francs. Comparison of these figures justifies informing the stockholders of that firm and the Deputies with a financial interest in alcohol that they have certainly killed more children than they think. As an opponent of capital punishment, I am far from asking that they be condemned to death. But, to begin with, it strikes me as indispensable and urgent to take them under military escort to the next execution of a murderer of children and to hand them on their way out a statistical report including the figures I have given.

The State that sows alcohol cannot be surprised to reap crime.[2] Instead of showing surprise, it simply goes on cutting off heads into which it has poured so much alcohol. It metes out justice imperturbably and poses as a creditor: its good conscience does not suffer at all. Witness the alcohol salesman who, in answer to the *Figaro's* inquiry, exclaimed: "I know just what the staunchest enemy of the death penalty would do if, having a weapon within reach, he suddenly saw assassins on the point of killing his father, his mother, his children, or his best friend. Well!" That "well" in itself seems somewhat alcoholized. Naturally, the staunchest enemy of capital

[2] The partisans of the death penalty made considerable publicity at the end of the last century about an increase in criminality beginning in 1880, which seemed to parallel a decrease in application of the penalty. But in 1880 a law was promulgated that permitted bars to be opened without any prior authorization. After that, just try to interpret statistics!

punishment would shoot those murderers, and rightly so, without thereby losing any of his reasons for staunchly defending abolition of the death penalty. But if he were to follow through his thinking and the afore-mentioned assassins reeked of alcohol, he would then go and take care of those whose vocation is to intoxicate future criminals. It is even quite surprising that the relatives of victims of alcoholic crimes have never thought of getting some enlightenment from the Parliament. Yet nothing of the sort takes place, and the State, enjoying general confidence, even supported by public opinion, goes on chastising assassins (particularly the alcoholics) somewhat in the way the pimp chastises the hard-working creatures who assure his livelihood. But the pimp at least does no moralizing. The State does. Although jurisprudence admits that drunkenness sometimes constitutes an extenuating circumstance, the State is ignorant of chronic alcoholism. Drunkenness, however, accompanies only crimes of violence, which are not punished with death, whereas the chronic alcoholic is capable also of premeditated crimes, which will bring about his death. Consequently, the State reserves the right to punish in the only case in which it has a real responsibility.

Does this amount to saying that every alcoholic must be declared irresponsible by a State that will beat its breast until the nation drinks nothing but fruit juice? Certainly not. No more than that the reasons based on heredity should cancel all culpability. The real responsibility of an offender cannot be precisely measured. We know that arithmetic is incapable of adding up the number of our antecedents, whether alcoholic or not. Going back to the beginning of time, the figure would be twenty-two times, raised to the tenth power, greater than the number of present inhabitants of the earth. The number of bad or morbid predispositions our antecedents have been able to transmit to us is, thus, incalculable. We come into the world laden with the weight of an infinite necessity. One would have to grant us, therefore, a general irresponsibility. Logic would demand that neither punishment nor reward should ever be meted out, and, by the same token, all society would become impossible. The instinct of preservation of societies, and hence of individuals, requires instead that individual responsibility be postulated and accepted without dreaming of an absolute indulgence that would amount to the death of all society. But the same reasoning must lead us to conclude that there never exists any total responsibility or, consequently, any absolute punishment or reward. No one can be rewarded completely, not even the winners of Nobel Prizes. But no one should be punished absolutely if he is thought guilty, and certainly not if there is a chance of his being innocent. The death penalty, which really neither provides an example nor assures distributive justice, simply usurps an exorbitant privilege by claiming to punish an always relative culpability by a definitive and irreparable punishment.

If indeed capital punishment represents a doubtful example and an unsatisfactory justice, we must agree with its defenders that it is eliminative. The death penalty definitively eliminates the condemned man. That alone, to tell the truth, ought to exclude, for its partisans especially, the repetition of risky arguments which, as we have just seen, can always be contested. Instead, one might frankly say that it is definitive because it must be, and affirm that certain men are irremediable in society, that they constitute a permanent danger for every citizen and for the social order, and that therefore, before anything else, they must be suppressed. No one, in any case, can refute the existence in society of certain wild animals whose energy and brutality nothing seems capable of breaking. The death penalty, to be sure, does not solve the problem they create. Let us agree, at least, that it suppresses the problem.

I shall come back to such men. But is capital punishment applied only to them? Is there any assurance that none of those executed is remediable? Can it even be asserted that none of them is innocent? In both cases, must it not be admitted that capital punishment is eliminative only insofar as it is irreparable? The 15th of March 1957, Burton Abbott was executed in California, condemned to death for having murdered a little girl of fourteen. Men who commit such a heinous crime are, I believe, classified among the irremediable. Although Abbott continually protested his innocence, he was condemned. His execution had been set for the 15th of March at ten o'clock. At 9:10 a delay was granted to allow his attorneys to make a final appeal.[3] At eleven o'clock the appeal was refused. At 11:15 Abbott entered

[3] It must be noted that the custom in American prisons is to move the condemned man into another cell on the eve of his execution while announcing to him the ceremony in store for him.

the gas chamber. At 11:18 he breathed in the first whiffs of gas. At 11:20 the secretary of the Committee on Reprieves called on the telephone. The Committee had changed its mind. They had tried to reach the Governor, who was out sailing; then they had phoned the prison directly. Abbott was taken from the gas chamber. It was too late. If only it had been cloudy over California that day, the Governor would not have gone out sailing. He would have telephoned two minutes earlier; today Abbott would be alive and would perhaps see his innocence proved. Any other penalty, even the harshest, would have left him that chance. The death penalty left him none.

This case is exceptional, some will say. Our lives are exceptional, too, and yet, in the fleeting existence that is ours, this takes place near us, at some ten hours' distance by air. Abbott's misfortune is less an exception than a news item like so many others, a mistake that is not isolated if we can believe our newspapers (see the Deshays case, to cite but the most recent one). The jurist Olivecroix, applying the law of probability to the chance of judicial error, around 1860, concluded that perhaps one innocent man was condemned in every two hundred and fifty-seven cases. The proportion is small? It is small in relation to average penalties. It is infinite in relation to capital punishment. When Hugo writes that to him the name of the guillotine is Lesurques,[4] he does not mean that all those who are decapitated are Lesurques, but that one Lesurques is enough for the

[4] This is the name of the innocent man guillotined in the case of the *Courrier de Lyon*.

guillotine to be permanently dishonored. It is under-standable that Belgium gave up once and for all pro-nouncing the death penalty after a judicial error and that England raised the question of abolition after the Hayes case. It is also possible to understand the conclu-sions of the Attorney General who, when consulted as to the appeal of a very probably guilty criminal whose victim had not been found, wrote: "The survival of X . . . gives the authorities the possibility of examining at leisure any new clue that might eventually be brought in as to the existence of his wife.[5] . . . On the other hand, the execution, by canceling that hypothetical possibility of examination, would, I fear, give to the slightest clue a theoretical value, a power of regret that I think it inop-portune to create." A love of justice and truth is ex-pressed here in a most moving way, and it would be ap-propriate to quote often in our courts that "power of re-gret" which so vividly sums up the danger that faces every juror. Once the innocent man is dead, no one can do anything for him, in fact, but to rehabilitate him, if there is still someone to ask for this. Then he is given back his innocence, which, to tell the truth, he had never lost. But the persecution of which he was a victim, his dreadful sufferings, his horrible death have been given him forever. It remains only to think of the innocent men of the future, so that these tortures may be spared them. This was done in Belgium. In France consciences are apparently untroubled.

Probably the French take comfort from the idea that

[5] The condemned man was accused of having killed his wife. But her body had not been found.

justice has progressed hand in hand with science. When
the learned expert holds forth in court, it seems as if a
priest has spoken, and the jury, raised in the religion of
science, expresses its opinion. However, recent cases,
chief among them the Besnard case, have shown us what
a comedy of experts is like. Culpability is no better established for having been established in a test tube, even
a graduated one. A second test tube will tell a different
story, and the personal equation loses none of its importance in such dangerous mathematics. The proportion
of learned men who are really experts is the same as that
of judges who are psychologists, hardly any greater than
that of serious and objective juries. Today, as yesterday,
the chance of error remains. Tomorrow another expert
testimony will declare the innocence of some Abbott or
other. But Abbott will be dead, scientifically dead, and
the science that claims to prove innocence as well as
guilt has not yet reached the point of resuscitating those
it kills.

Among the guilty themselves, is there any assurance
that none but the irretrievable have been killed? All
those who, like me, have at a period of their lives necessarily followed the assize courts know that a large element of chance enters into any sentence. The look of the
accused, his antecedents (adultery is often looked upon
as an aggravating circumstance by jurors who may or
may not all have been always faithful), his manner
(which is in his favor only if it is conventional—in other
words, play-acting most of the time), his very elocution
(the old hands know that one must neither stammer nor
be too eloquent), the mishaps of the trial enjoyed in a

sentimental key (and the truth, alas, is not always emo-
tionally effective): so many flukes that influence the final decision of the jury. At the moment of the death
verdict, one may be sure that to arrive at the most definite
of penalties, an extraordinary combination of uncertainties was necessary. When it is known that the supreme
verdict depends on the jury's evaluation of the extenuating circumstances, when it is known, above all, that the
reform of 1832 gave our juries the power of granting
indeterminate extenuating circumstances, it is possible
to imagine the latitude left to the passing mood of the
jurors. The law no longer foresees precisely the cases in
which death is to be the outcome; so the jury decides
after the event by guesswork. Inasmuch as there are
never two comparable juries, the man who is executed
might well not have been. Beyond reclaim in the eyes of
the respectable people of Ille-et-Vilaine, he would have
been granted a semblance of excuse by the good citizens
of the Var. Unfortunately, the same blade falls in the
two Départements. And it makes no distinction.

The temporal risks are added to the geographical risks
to increase the general absurdity. The French Communist workman who has just been guillotined in Algeria
for having put a bomb (discovered before it went off) in
a factory locker room was condemned as much because
of the general climate as because of what he did. In the
present state of mind in Algeria, there was a desire at
one and the same time to prove to the Arab opinion that
the guillotine was designed for Frenchmen too and to
satisfy the French opinion wrought up by the crimes of
terrorism. At the same moment, however, the Minister

who approved the execution was accepting Communist votes in his electoral district. If the circumstances had been different, the accused would have got off easy and his only risk, once he had become a Deputy of the party, would be finding himself having a drink at the same bar as the Minister someday. Such thoughts are bitter, and one would like them to remain alive in the minds of our leaders. They must know that times and customs change; a day comes when the guilty man, too rapidly executed, does not seem so black. But it is too late and there is no alternative but to repent or to forget. Of course, people forget. Nonetheless, society is no less affected. The unpunished crime, according to the Greeks, infected the whole city. But innocence condemned or crime too severely punished, in the long run, soils the city just as much. We know this, in France.

Such, it will be said, is human justice, and, despite its imperfections, it is better than arbitrariness. But that sad evaluation is bearable only in connection with ordinary penalties. It is scandalous in the face of verdicts of death. A classic treatise on French law, in order to excuse the death penalty for not involving degrees, states this: "Human justice has not the slightest desire to assure such a proportion. Why? Because it knows it is frail." Must we therefore conclude that such frailty authorizes us to pronounce an absolute judgment and that, uncertain of ever achieving pure justice, society must rush headlong, through the greatest risks, toward supreme injustice? If justice admits that it is frail, would it not be better for justice to be modest and to allow its judgments sufficient latitude so that a mistake can be corrected? [6] Could not justice concede to the criminal the same weakness in which society finds a sort of permanent extenuating circumstance for itself? Can the jury decently say: "If I kill you by mistake, you will forgive me when you consider the weaknesses of our common nature. But I am condemning you to death without considering those weaknesses or that nature"? There is a solidarity of all men in error and aberration. Must that solidarity operate for the tribunal and be denied the accused? No, and if justice has any meaning in this world, it means nothing but the recognition of that solidarity; it cannot, by its very essence, divorce itself from compassion. Compassion, of course, can in this instance be but awareness of a common suffering and not a frivolous indulgence paying no attention to the sufferings and rights of the victim. Compassion does not exclude punishment, but it suspends the final condemnation. Compassion loathes the definitive, irreparable measure that does an injustice to mankind as a whole because of failing to take into account the wretchedness of the common condition.

To tell the truth, certain juries are well aware of this, for they often admit extenuating circumstances in a crime that nothing can extenuate. This is because the death penalty seems excessive to them in such cases and

[6] We congratulated ourselves on having reprieved Sillon, who recently killed his four-year-old daughter in order not to give her to her mother, who wanted a divorce. It was discovered, in fact, during his imprisonment that Sillon was suffering from a brain tumor that might explain the madness of his deed.

they prefer not punishing enough to punishing too much. The extreme severity of the penalty then favors crime instead of penalizing it. There is not a court session during which we do not read in the press that a verdict is incoherent and that, in view of the facts, it seems either insufficient or excessive. But the jurors are not ignorant of this. However, faced with the enormity of capital punishment, they prefer, as we too should prefer, to look like fools rather than to compromise their nights to come. Knowing themselves to be fallible, they at least draw the appropriate consequences. And true justice is on their side precisely insofar as logic is not.

There are, however, major criminals whom all juries would condemn at any time and in any place whatever. Their crimes are not open to doubt, and the evidence brought by the accusation is confirmed by the confessions of the defense. Most likely, everything that is abnormal and monstrous in them is enough to classify them as pathological. But the psychiatric experts, in the majority of cases, affirm their responsibility. Recently in Paris a young man, somewhat weak in character but kind and affectionate, devoted to his family, was, according to his own admission, annoyed by a remark his father made about his coming home late. The father was sitting reading at the dining-room table. The young man seized an ax and dealt his father several blows from behind. Then in the same way he struck down his mother, who was in the kitchen. He undressed, hid his bloodstained trousers in the closet, went to make a call on the family of his fiancée, without showing any signs, then returned home and notified the police that he had just found his parents murdered. The police immediately discovered the bloodstained trousers and, without difficulty, got a calm confession from the parricide. The psychiatrists decided that this man who murdered through annoyance was responsible. His odd indifference, of which he was to give other indications in prison (showing pleasure because his parents' funeral had attracted so many people—"They were much loved," he told his lawyer), cannot, however, be considered as normal. But his reasoning power was apparently untouched.

Many "monsters" offer equally impenetrable exteriors. They are eliminated on the mere consideration of the facts. Apparently the nature or the magnitude of their crimes allows no room for imagining that they can ever repent or reform. They must merely be kept from doing it again, and there is no other solution but to eliminate them. On this frontier, and on it alone, discussion about the death penalty is legitimate. In all other cases the arguments for capital punishment do not stand up to the criticisms of the abolitionists. But in extreme cases, and in our state of ignorance, we make a wager. No fact, no reasoning can bring together those who think that a chance must always be left to the vilest of men and those who consider that chance illusory. But it is perhaps possible, on that final frontier, to go beyond the long opposition between partisans and adversaries of the death penalty by weighing the advisability of that penalty today, and in Europe. With much less competence, I shall try to reply to the wish expressed by a Swiss jurist, Professor Jean Graven, who wrote in 1952 in his remarkable study on the problem of the death penalty: "Faced with the problem that is once more confronting our conscience and our reason, we think that a solution must be sought, not through the conceptions, problems, and arguments of the past, nor through the hopes and theoretical promises of the future, but through the ideas, recognized facts, and necessities of the present." [7] It is possible, indeed, to debate endlessly as to the benefits or harm attributable to the death penalty through the ages or in an intellectual vacuum. But it plays a role here and now, and we must take our stand here and now in relation to the modern executioner. What does the death penalty mean to the men of the mid-century?

To simplify matters, let us say that our civilization has lost the only values that, in a certain way, can justify that penalty and, on the other hand, suffers from evils that necessitate its suppression. In other words, the abolition of the death penalty ought to be asked for by all thinking members of our society, for reasons both of logic and of realism.

Of logic, to begin with. Deciding that a man must have the definitive punishment imposed on him is tantamount to deciding that that man has no chance of making amends. This is the point, to repeat ourselves, where the arguments clash blindly and crystallize in a sterile opposition. But it so happens that none among us can settle the question, for we are all both judges and interested parties. Whence our uncertainty as to our right to kill and our inability to convince each other.

[7] *Revue de Criminologie et de Police Technique* (Geneva), special issue, 1952.

Without absolute innocence, there is no supreme judge. Now, we have all done wrong in our lives even if that wrong, without falling within the jurisdiction of the laws, went as far as the unknown crime. There are no just people—merely hearts more or less lacking in justice. Living at least allows us to discover this and to add to the sum of our actions a little of the good that will make up in part for the evil we have added to the world. Such a right to live, which allows a chance to make amends, is the natural right of every man, even the worst man. The lowest of criminals and the most up-right of judges meet side by side, equally wretched in their solidarity. Without that right, moral life is utterly impossible. None among us is authorized to despair of a single man, except after his death, which transforms his life into destiny and then permits a definitive judgment. But pronouncing the definitive judgment before his death, decreeing the closing of accounts when the creditor is still alive, is no man's right. On this limit, at least, whoever judges absolutely condemns himself absolutely.

Bernard Fallot of the Masuy gang, working for the Gestapo, was condemned to death after admitting the many terrible crimes of which he was guilty, and declared himself that he could not be pardoned. "My hands are too red with blood," he told a prison mate.[8] Public opinion and the opinion of his judges certainly classed him among the irremediable, and I should have been tempted to agree if I had not read a surprising

[8] Jean Bocognano: *Quartier des fauves, prison de Fresnes* (Editions du Fuseau).

testimony. This is what Fallot said to the same companion after declaring that he wanted to die courageously: "Shall I tell you my greatest regret? Well, it is not having known the Bible I now have here. I assure you that I wouldn't be where I now am." There is no question of giving in to some conventional set of sentimental pictures and calling to mind Victor Hugo's good convicts. The age of enlightenment, as people say, wanted to suppress the death penalty on the pretext that man was naturally good. Of course he is not (he is worse or better). After twenty years of our magnificent history we are well aware of this. But precisely because he is not absolutely good, no one among us can pose as an absolute judge and pronounce the definitive elimination of the worst among the guilty, because no one of us can lay claim to absolute innocence. Capital judgment upsets the only indisputable human solidarity—our solidarity against death—and it can be legitimized only by a truth or a principle that is superior to man.

In fact, the supreme punishment has always been, throughout the ages, a religious penalty. Inflicted in the name of the king, God's representative on earth, or by priests or in the name of society considered as a sacred body, it denies, not human solidarity, but the guilty man's membership in the divine community, the only thing that can give him life. Life on earth is taken from him, to be sure, but his chance of making amends is left him. The real judgment is not pronounced; it will be in the other world. Only religious values, and especially belief in eternal life, can therefore serve as a basis for the supreme punishment because, according to their own logic, they keep it from being definitive and irreparable. Consequently, it is justified only insofar as it is not supreme.

The Catholic Church, for example, has always accepted the necessity of the death penalty. It inflicted that penalty itself, and without stint, in other periods. Even today it justifies it and grants the State the right to apply it. The Church's position, however subtle, contains a very deep feeling that was expressed directly in 1937 by a Swiss National Councillor from Fribourg during a discussion in the National Council. According to M. Grand, the lowest of criminals when faced with execution withdraws into himself. "He repents and his preparation for death is thereby facilitated. The Church has saved one of its members and fulfilled its divine mission. This is why it has always accepted the death penalty, not only as a means of self-defense, but *as a powerful means of salvation.*[9] . . . Without trying to make of it a thing of the Church, the death penalty can point proudly to its almost divine efficacy, like war."

By virtue of the same reasoning, probably, there could be read on the sword of the Fribourg executioner the words: "Lord Jesus, thou art the judge." Hence the executioner is invested with a sacred function. He is the man who destroys the body in order to deliver the soul to the divine sentence, which no one can judge beforehand. Some may think that such words imply rather scandalous confusions. And, to be sure, whoever clings to the teaching of Jesus will look upon that handsome sword as one more outrage to the person of Christ. In the

[9] My italics.

light of this, it is possible to understand the dreadful remark of the Russian condemned man about to be hanged by the Tsar's executioners in 1905 who said firmly to the priest who had come to console him with the image of Christ: "Go away and commit no sacrilege." The unbeliever cannot keep from thinking that men who have set at the center of their faith the staggering victim of a judicial error ought at least to hesitate before committing legal murder. Believers might also be reminded that Emperor Julian, before his conversion, did not want to give official offices to Christians because they systematically refused to pronounce death sentences or to have anything to do with them. For five centuries Christians therefore believed that the strict moral teaching of their master forbade killing. But Catholic faith is not nourished solely by the personal teaching of Christ. It also feeds on the Old Testament, on St. Paul, and on the Church Fathers. In particular, the immortality of the soul and the universal resurrection of bodies are articles of dogma. As a result, capital punishment is for the believer a temporary penalty that leaves the final sentence in suspense, an arrangement necessary only for terrestrial order, an administrative measure which, far from signifying the end for the guilty man, may instead favor his redemption. I am not saying that all believers agree with this, and I can readily imagine that some Catholics may stand closer to Christ than to Moses or St. Paul. I am simply saying that faith in the immortality of the soul allowed Catholicism to see the problem of capital punishment in very different terms and to justify it.

But what is the value of such a justification in the society we live in, which in its institutions and its customs has lost all contact with the sacred? When an atheistic or skeptical or agnostic judge inflicts the death penalty on an unbelieving criminal, he is pronouncing a definitive punishment that cannot be reconsidered. He takes his place on the throne of God,[1] without having the same powers and even without believing in God. He kills, in short, because his ancestors believed in eternal life. But the society that he claims to represent is in reality pronouncing a simple measure of elimination, doing violence to the human community united against death, and taking a stand as an absolute value because society is laying claim to absolute power. To be sure, it delegates a priest to the condemned man, through tradition. The priest may legitimately hope that fear of punishment will help the guilty man's conversion. Who can accept, however, that such a calculation should justify a penalty most often inflicted and received in a quite different spirit? It is one thing to believe before being afraid and another to find faith after fear. Conversion through fire or the guillotine will always be suspect, and it may seem surprising that the Church has not given up conquering infidels through terror. In any case, society that has lost all contact with the sacred can find no advantage in a conversion in which it professes to have no interest. Society decrees a sacred punishment and at the same time divests it both of excuse and of usefulness. Society proceeds sovereignly to eliminate the

[1] As everyone knows, the jury's decision is preceded by the words: "Before God and my conscience. . . ."

evil ones from her midst as if she were virtue itself. Like an honorable man killing his wayward son and remarking: "Really, I didn't know what to do with him." She assumes the right to select as if she were nature herself and to add great sufferings to the elimination as if she were a redeeming god.

To assert, in any case, that a man must be absolutely cut off from society because he is absolutely evil amounts to saying that society is absolutely good, and no one in his right mind will believe this today. Instead of believing this, people will more readily think the reverse. Our society has become so bad and so criminal only because she has respected nothing but her own preservation or a good reputation in history. Society has indeed lost all contact with the sacred. But society began in the nineteenth century to find a substitute for religion by proposing herself as an object of adoration. The doctrines of evolution and the notions of selection that accompany them have made of the future of society a final end. The political utopias that were grafted onto those doctrines placed at the end of time a golden age that justified in advance any enterprises whatever. Society became accustomed to legitimizing what might serve her future and, consequently, to making use of the supreme punishment in an absolute way. From then on, society considered as a crime and a sacrilege anything that stood in the way of her plan and her temporal dogmas. In other words, after being a priest, the executioner became a government official. The result is here all around us. The situation is such that this mid-century society which has lost the right, in all logic, to decree capital punishment ought now to suppress it for reasons of realism.

In relation to crime, how can our civilization be defined? The reply is easy: for thirty years now, State crimes have been far more numerous than individual crimes. I am not even speaking of wars, general or localized, although bloodshed too is an alcohol that eventually intoxicates like the headiest of wines. But the number of individuals killed directly by the State has assumed astronomical proportions and infinitely outnumbers private murders. There are fewer and fewer condemned by common law and more and more condemned for political reasons. The proof is that each of us, however honorable he may be, can foresee the possibility of being someday condemned to death, whereas that eventuality would have seemed ridiculous at the beginning of the century. Alphonse Karr's witty remark: "Let the noble assassins begin" has no meaning now. Those who cause the most blood to flow are the same ones who believe they have right, logic, and history on their side.

Hence our society must now defend herself not so much against the individual as against the State. It may be that the proportions will be reversed in another thirty years. But, for the moment, our self-defense must be aimed at the State first and foremost. Justice and expediency command the law to protect the individual against a State given over to the follies of sectarianism or of pride. "Let the State begin and abolish the death penalty" ought to be our rallying cry today.

Bloodthirsty laws, it has been said, make bloodthirsty

customs. But any society eventually reaches a state of
ignominy in which, despite every disorder, the customs
never manage to be as bloodthirsty as the laws. Half of
Europe knows that condition. We French knew it in the
past and may again know it. Those executed during the
Occupation led to those executed at the time of the
Liberation, whose friends now dream of revenge. Elsewhere States laden with too many crimes are getting
ready to drown their guilt in even greater massacres.
One kills for a nation or a class that has been granted
divine status. One kills for a future society that has likewise been given divine status. Whoever thinks he has
omniscience imagines he has omnipotence. Temporal
idols demanding an absolute faith tirelessly decree absolute punishments. And religions devoid of transcend-
ence kill great numbers of condemned men devoid of
hope.

How can European society of the mid-century survive
unless it decides to defend individuals by every means
against the State's oppression? Forbidding a man's
execution would amount to proclaiming publicly that
society and the State are not absolute values, that nothing
authorizes them to legislate definitively or to bring about
the irreparable. Without the death penalty, Gabriel
Péri and Brasillach would perhaps be among us. We
could then judge them according to our opinion and
proudly proclaim our judgment, whereas now they judge
us and we keep silent. Without the death penalty Rajk's
corpse would not poison Hungary; Germany, with less
guilt on her conscience, would be more favorably looked
upon by Europe; the Russian Revolution would not be

agonizing in shame; and Algerian blood would weigh less heavily on our consciences. Without the death penalty, Europe would not be infected by the corpses accumulated for the last twenty years in its tired soil. On our continent, all values are upset by fear and hatred between individuals and between nations. In the conflict of ideas the weapons are the cord and the guillotine. A natural and human society exercising her right of repression has given way to a dominant ideology that requires human sacrifices. "The example of the gallows," it has been written,[2] "is that a man's life ceases to be sacred when it is thought useful to kill him." Apparently it is becoming ever more useful; the example is being copied; the contagion is spreading everywhere. And together with it, the disorder of nihilism. Hence we must call a spectacular halt and proclaim, in our principles and institutions, that the individual is above the State. And any measure that decreases the pressure of social forces upon the individual will help to relieve the congestion of a Europe suffering from a rush of blood, allowing us to think more clearly and to start on the way toward health. Europe's malady consists in believing nothing and claiming to know everything. But Europe is far from knowing everything, and, judging from the revolt and hope we feel, she believes in something: she believes that the extreme of man's wretchedness, on some mysterious limit, borders on the extreme of his greatness. For the majority of Europeans, faith is lost. And with it, the justifications faith provided in the domain of punishment. But the majority of Europeans also reject the State

[2] By Francart.

idolatry that aimed to take the place of faith. Henceforth in mid-course, both certain and uncertain, having made up our minds never to submit and never to oppress, we should admit at one and the same time our hope and our ignorance, we should refuse absolute law and the irreparable judgment. We know enough to say that this or that major criminal deserves hard labor for life. But we don't know enough to decree that he be shorn of his future—in other words, of the chance we all have of making amends. Because of what I have just said, in the unified Europe of the future the solemn abolition of the death penalty ought to be the first article of the European Code we all hope for.

From the humanitarian idylls of the eighteenth century to the bloodstained gallows the way leads directly, and the executioners of today, as everyone knows, are humanists. Hence we cannot be too wary of the humanitarian ideology in dealing with a problem such as the death penalty. On the point of concluding, I should like therefore to repeat that neither an illusion as to the natural goodness of the human being nor faith in a golden age to come motivates my opposition to the death penalty. On the contrary, its abolition seems to me necessary because of reasoned pessimism, of logic, and of realism. Not that the heart has no share in what I have said. Anyone who has spent weeks with texts, recollections, and men having any contact, whether close or not, with the gallows could not possibly remain untouched by that experience. But, let me repeat, I do not believe, nonetheless, that there is no responsibility in this world and that we must give way to that modern tendency to absolve everything, victim and murderer, in the same confusion. Such purely sentimental confusion is made up of cowardice rather than of generosity and eventually justifies whatever is worst in this world. If you keep on excusing, you eventually give your blessing to the slave camp, to cowardly force, to organized executioners, to the cynicism of great political monsters; you finally hand over your brothers. This can be seen around us. But it so happens, in the present state of the world, that the man of today wants laws and institutions suitable to a convalescent, which will curb him without breaking him and lead him without crushing him. Hurled into the unchecked dynamic movement of history, he needs a natural philosophy and a few laws of equilibrium. He needs, in short, a society based on reason and not the anarchy into which he has been plunged by his own pride and the excessive powers of the State.

I am convinced that abolition of the death penalty would help us progress toward that society. After taking such an initiative, France could offer to extend it to the non-abolitionist countries on both sides of the iron curtain. But, in any case, she should set the example. Capital punishment would then be replaced by hard labor—for life in the case of criminals considered irremediable and for a fixed period in the case of the others. To any who feel that such a penalty is harsher than capital punishment we can only express our amazement that they did not suggest, in this case, reserving it for such as Landru and applying capital punishment to minor criminals. We might remind them, too, that hard labor leaves the condemned man the possibility of choosing death, whereas the guillotine offers no alternative. To any who feel, on the other hand, that hard labor is too mild a penalty, we can answer first that they lack imagination and secondly that privation of freedom seems to them a slight punishment only insofar as contemporary society has taught us to despise freedom.[3]

The fact that Cain is not killed but bears a mark of reprobation in the eyes of men is the lesson we must draw from the Old Testament, to say nothing of the Gospels, instead of looking back to the cruel examples of the Mosaic law. In any case, nothing keeps us from trying out an experiment, limited in duration (ten years, for instance), if our Parliament is still incapable of making up for its votes in favor of alcohol by such a great civilizing step as complete abolition of the penalty. And if, really, public opinion and its representatives cannot give up the law of laziness which simply eliminates what it cannot reform, let us at least—while hoping for a new day of truth—not make of it the "solemn

[3] See the report on the death penalty by Representative Dupont in the National Assembly on 31 May 1791: "A sharp and burning mood consumes the assassin; the thing he fears most is inactivity; it leaves him to himself, and to get away from it he continually braves death and tries to cause death in others; solitude and his own conscience are his real torture. Does this not suggest to you what kind of punishment should be inflicted on him, what is the kind to which he will be most sensitive? *Is it not in the nature of the malady that the remedy is to be found?*" I have italicized the last sentence, for it makes of that little-known Representative a true precursor of our modern psychology.

slaughterhouse" [4] that befouls our society. The death penalty as it is now applied, and however rarely it may be, is a revolting butchery, an outrage inflicted on the person and body of man. That truncation, that living and yet uprooted head, those spurts of blood date from a barbarous period that aimed to impress the masses with degrading sights. Today when such vile death is administered on the sly, what is the meaning of this torture? The truth is that in the nuclear age we kill as we did in the age of the spring balance. And there is not a man of normal sensitivity who, at the mere thought of such crude surgery, does not feel nauseated. If the French State is incapable of overcoming habit and giving Europe one of the remedies it needs, let France begin by reforming the manner of administering capital punishment. The science that serves to kill so many could at least serve to kill decently. An anesthetic that would allow the condemned man to slip from sleep to death (which would be left within his reach for at least a day so that he could use it freely and would be administered to him in another form if he were unwilling or weak of will) would assure his elimination, if you insist, but would put a little decency into what is at present but a sordid and obscene exhibition.

I suggest such compromises only insofar as one must occasionally despair of seeing wisdom and true civilization influence those responsible for our future. For certain men, more numerous than we think, it is physically unbearable to know what the death penalty really is and not to be able to prevent its application. In their way,

[4] Tarde.

they suffer that penalty themselves, and without any justice. If only the weight of filthy images weighing upon them were reduced, society would lose nothing. But even that, in the long run, will be inadequate. There will be no lasting peace either in the heart of individuals or in social customs until death is outlawed.

THE ARTIST
AND HIS TIME

THE WAGER OF OUR GENERATION

(Interview in *Demain,* issue of 24–30 October 1957)

The notion of art for art's sake is obviously alien to your thinking. That of "commitment" as it has been made fashionable of late is equally so. Taken in its present meaning, commitment consists in making one's art subservient to a policy. It seems to me that there is something more important, which is characteristic of your work, that might be called inserting that work into its time. Is this correct? And, if it is, how would you describe that insertion?

I CAN accept your expression: inserting a work into its time. But, after all, this describes all literary art. Every writer tries to give a form to the passions of his time. Yesterday it was love. Today the great passions of unity and liberty disrupt the world. Yesterday love led to individual death. Today collective passions make us run the risk of universal destruction. Today, just as yesterday, art wants to save from death a living image of our passions and our sufferings.

Perhaps it is harder today. It is possible to fall in love every once in a while. Once is enough, after all. But it is not possible to be a militant in one's spare time. And so the artist of today becomes unreal if he remains in his ivory tower or sterilized if he spends his time galloping around the political arena. Yet between the two lies the arduous way of true art. It seems to me that the writer must be fully aware of the dramas of his time and that he must take sides every time he can or knows how to do so. But he must also maintain or resume from time to time a certain distance in relation to our history. Every work presupposes a content of reality and a creator who shapes the container. Consequently, the artist, if he must share the misfortune of his time, must also tear himself away in order to consider that misfortune and give it form. This continual shuttling, this tension that gradually becomes increasingly dangerous, is the task of the artist of today. Perhaps this means that in a short time there will be no more artists. And perhaps not. It is a question of time, of strength, of mastery, and also of chance.

In any case, this is what ought to be. There remains what is; there remains the truth of our days, which is less magnificent. And the truth, as I see it at least, is that the artist is groping his way in the dark, just like the man in the street—incapable of separating himself from the world's misfortune and passionately longing for solitude and silence; dreaming of justice, yet being himself a source of injustice; dragged—even though he thinks he is driving it—behind a chariot that is bigger than he. In this exhausting adventure the artist can only draw help from others, and, like anyone else, he will get help from pleasure, from forgetting, and also from friendship and admiration. And, like anyone else, he will get help from hope. In my case, I have always drawn my hope from the idea of fecundity. Like many men today, I am tired of criticism, of disparagement, of spitefulness—of nihilism, in short. It is essential to condemn what must be condemned, but swiftly and firmly. On the other hand, one should praise at length what still deserves to be praised. After all, that is why I am an artist, because even the work that negates still affirms something and does homage to the wretched and magnificent life that is ours.

> When a man speaks as you do, he is not speaking solely for himself. He is inevitably speaking for others. And he is speaking for something. In other words, he is speaking in the name of and in favor of men for whom those values count. Who are those men and what are those values?

To begin with, I feel a solidarity with the common man. Tomorrow the world may burst into fragments. In that threat hanging over our heads there is a lesson of truth. As we face such a future, hierarchies, titles, honors are reduced to what they are in reality: a passing puff of smoke. And the only certainty left to us is that of naked suffering, common to all, intermingling its roots with those of a stubborn hope.

In the battles of our time I have always been on the side of the obstinate, on the side of those who have never despaired of a certain honor. I have shared and I still share many of the contemporary frenzies. But I have never been able to get myself to spit, as so many others do, on the word "honor." Doubtless because I was and am aware of my human weaknesses and of my injustices, because I instinctively knew and still know that honor (like pity) is an unreasonable virtue that takes the place of justice and reason, which have become powerless. The man whose blood, and extravagances, and frail heart lead him to the commonest weaknesses must rely on something in order to get to the point of respecting himself and hence of respecting others. This is why I loathe a certain self-satisfied virtue, I loathe society's dreadful morality because it results, exactly like absolute cynicism, in making men despair and in keeping them from taking responsibility for their own life with all its weight of errors and greatness.

The aim of art, the aim of a life can only be to increase the sum of freedom and responsibility to be found in every man and in the world. It cannot, under any circumstances, be to reduce or suppress that freedom, even temporarily. There are works of art that tend to make man conform and to convert him to some external rule. Others tend to subject him to whatever is worst in him, to terror or hatred. Such works are valueless to me. No great work has ever been based on hatred or contempt. On the contrary, there is not a single true work of art that has not in the end added to the inner freedom of each person who has known and loved it. Yes, that is the freedom I am extolling, and it is what helps me through life. An artist may make a success or a failure of his work. He may make a success or a failure of his life. But if he can tell himself that, finally, as a result of his long effort, he has eased or decreased the various forms of bondage weighing upon men, then in a sense he is justified and, to some extent, he can forgive himself.

At the source of every work there is an experience. It may be a brief and brutal experience, a trauma. It may also be a protracted experience, generally the experience of childhood and adolescence. For you, to begin with, there was the Mediterranean and poverty. But with maturity come other experiences to influence and color one's early impressions. For you they took the form of war and Resistance. Have not the last few years likewise been the source of a new experience? In what way, and what have they brought you?

Yes, there was the sun and poverty. Then sports, from which I learned all I know about ethics. Next the war and the Resistance. And, as a result, the temptation of hatred. Seeing beloved friends and relatives killed is not a schooling in generosity. The temptation of hatred had to be overcome. And I did so. This is an experience that counts.

Then the years since the Liberation were largely marked, in my case, by the experience of a solitary struggle. I had friends, to be sure, good, generous, and loyal friends, the mere thought of whom warms my heart today. But the decisions I had to make, which counted the most for me—the decision to write *The Rebel,* for instance—were solitary and difficult decisions. And also what followed. But at the same time history progressed. East Berlin, Poznan, Budapest . . . A gigantic myth collapsed. A certain truth, which had long been disguised, burst upon the world. And if the present is still spattered with blood and the future still dark, at least we know that the era of ideologies is over, and the force of resistance, together with the value of freedom, gives us new reasons for living.

That's it. And of course one must add purely personal experiences.

We spoke of inserting a work into its time. But it also belongs to a current of thought that is, in a way, geographical. It strikes me that your work, like that of several contemporary writers

—I am thinking particularly
of Silone and Ortega y Gasset—can be said to belong to
Europe. Are you aware of
this and does that intellectual Europe seem to you a
reality?

Yes, I am aware of such a Europe and I believe it fore-
shadows our political future. The more French I feel, the
more I believe this. No one is more closely attached to
his Algerian province than I, and yet I have no trouble
feeling a part of French tradition. Consequently, I
learned, as naturally as we learn to breathe, that love of
one's native land can broaden without dying. And,
finally, it is because I love my country that I feel
European. Just take for example Ortega y Gasset, whom
you were right to mention. He is perhaps the greatest of
European writers after Nietzsche, and yet it would be
hard to be more Spanish. Silone speaks to all of Europe,
and the reason I feel so close to him is that he is also
so unbelievably rooted in his national and even provincial tradition.

Unity and diversity, and never one without the other
—isn't this the very secret of our Europe? Europe has
lived on its contradictions, flourished on its differences,
and, constantly transcending itself thereby, has created
a civilization on which the whole world depends even
when rejecting it. This is why I do not believe in a
Europe unified under the weight of an ideology or of a
technocracy that would overlook these differences. Any
more than I believe in a Europe left to its differences

alone—in other words, left to an anarchy of enemy nationalisms.

If Europe is not destroyed by fire, it will come into being. And Russia will in time be added to it, with its individual differences. It will take more than Mr. Khrushchev to make me forget what links us to Tolstoy, to Dostoevsky, and to their people. But that future is threatened by war. Let me repeat, this is our wager. But it is one of the few wagers worth accepting.

You are an Algerian French writer. This is indeed what you made a point of emphasizing when you were awarded the Nobel Prize. But when you are aware of being an Algerian Frenchman, certainly you are not defining yourself by opposition to Algerians not of French origin. Albert Camus, a Frenchman from Algeria—doesn't this mean that you feel a solidarity with all Algerians? How can this be and how does that Algeria fit into the spiritual Europe to which you are also aware of belonging?

My role in Algeria never has been and never will be to divide, but rather to use whatever means I have to unite. I feel a solidarity with everyone, French or Arab, who is suffering today in the misfortune of my country. But I cannot all alone rebuild what so many men persist in destroying. I have done what I could. I shall begin again when there is again a chance of helping to rebuild an Algeria freed from all hatreds and all forms of racism. But, to limit ourselves to the domain we have chosen, I merely want to remind you that, simply by virtue of a generous interchange and a real solidarity, we have built up a community of Algerian writers, both French and Arab writers. That community is cut in two, for the time being. But men like Feraoun, Mammeri, Chraïbi, Dib, and so many others have taken their place among European writers. Whatever the future may be, and however dark it looks to me, I am sure that this cannot be forgotten.

Frequently when speaking of French culture you have used the word "rebirth." Not only do you wish for it, but it also seems that at times you perceive its first promise. What may be the form of that rebirth? What are the signs of it?

The change in generations taking place on all levels is one of the first signs. The quality of the new generation is another, as well as the increasing unwillingness to adopt slogans or ideologies and the return to less pretentious and more tangible values.

Europe (and France) has not yet emerged from fifty

years of nihilism. But the moment people begin rejecting the mystifications on which that nihilism is based,
then hope is possible. The whole question is to know
whether or not we shall develop faster than the rocket
with a nuclear warhead. And, unfortunately, the fruits
of the spirit are slower to ripen than intercontinental
missiles. But, after all, since atomic war would divest any
future of its meaning, it gives us complete freedom of
action. We have nothing to lose except everything. So
let's go ahead. This is the wager of our generation. If we
are to fail, it is better, in any case, to have stood on the
side of those who choose life than on the side of those
who are destroying.

> In all your work there co-
> exist philosophical pessimism
> and, nonetheless, not opti-
> mism but a sort of confi-
> dence. Confidence in the
> spirit rather than in man, in
> nature rather than in the uni-
> verse, in action rather than
> in its results. Do you think
> this attitude—which is that
> of the rebel, for the value of
> the revolt makes up for the
> world's absurdity—can be
> adopted by the majority or is
> it condemned to remain the
> privilege of a few wise men?

Is that position really so special? And do not the men
of today, threatened and yet resisting, live in this

manner? We stifle and yet survive, we think we are dying of grief and yet life wins out. The men of our time, whom we encounter in the streets, show in their faces that they know. The only difference is that some of them show more courage. Besides, we have no choice. It is either that or nihilism. If our societies must plunge into nihilism, whether totalitarian or bourgeois, then those individuals who refuse to give in will stand apart, and they must accept this. But in their place and within their means, they must do what is necessary so that all can live together again.

Personally, I have never wanted to stand apart. For the man of today there is a sort of solitude, which is certainly the harshest thing our era forces upon us. I feel its weight, believe me. But, nevertheless, I should not want to change eras, for I also know and respect the greatness of this one. Moreover, I have always thought that the maximum danger implied the maximum hope.

> One cannot avoid tackling certain subjects today. The most serious one is a problem for all men: in the struggles dividing the world today, must we really be willing to forget all that is bad on one side to fight what is worse on the other?

Before he died in combat in the last war, Richard Hilary found the phrase that sums up this dilemma:

"We were fighting a lie in the name of a half-truth."
He thought he was expressing a very pessimistic idea.
But one may even have to fight a lie in the name of a
quarter-truth. This is our situation at present. However,
the quarter-truth contained in Western society is called
liberty. And liberty is the way, and the only way, of
perfectibility. Without liberty heavy industry can be
perfected, but not justice or truth. Our most recent
history, from Berlin to Budapest, ought to convince us
of this. In any case, it is the reason for my choice. I have
said in this very place that none of the evils totalitarianism claims to remedy is worse than totalitarianism itself.
I have not changed my mind. On the contrary, after
twenty years of our harsh history, during which I have
tried to accept every experience it offered, liberty ultimately seems to me, for societies and for individuals,
for labor and for culture, the supreme good that governs
all others.

CREATE DANGEROUSLY

(Lecture given at the University of Uppsala in December 1957)

AN ORIENTAL wise man always used to ask the divinity in his prayers to be so kind as to spare him from living in an interesting era. As we are not wise, the divinity has not spared us and we are living in an interesting era. In any case, our era forces us to take an interest in it. The writers of today know this. If they speak up, they are criticized and attacked. If they become modest and keep silent, they are vociferously blamed for their silence.

In the midst of such din the writer cannot hope to remain aloof in order to pursue the reflections and images that are dear to him. Until the present moment, remaining aloof has always been possible in history. When someone did not approve, he could always keep silent or talk of something else. Today everything is changed and even silence has dangerous implications. The moment that abstaining from choice is itself looked upon as a choice and punished or praised as such, the artist is willy-nilly impressed into service. "Impressed" seems to me a more accurate term in this connection than "committed." Instead of signing up, indeed, for

voluntary service, the artist does his compulsory service.
Every artist today is embarked on the contemporary
slave galley. He has to resign himself to this even if he
considers that the galley reeks of its past, that the slave-
drivers are really too numerous, and, in addition, that
the steering is badly handled. We are on the high seas.
The artist, like everyone else, must bend to his oar,
without dying if possible—in other words, go on living
and creating.

To tell the truth, it is not easy, and I can understand
why artists regret their former comfort. The change is
somewhat cruel. Indeed, history's amphitheater has always contained the martyr and the lion. The former
relied on eternal consolations and the latter on raw
historical meat. But until now the artist was on the sidelines. He used to sing purposely, for his own sake, or
at best to encourage the martyr and make the lion forget
his appetite. But now the artist is in the amphitheater.
Of necessity, his voice is not quite the same; it is not
nearly so firm.

It is easy to see all that art can lose from such a constant obligation. Ease, to begin with, and that divine
liberty so apparent in the work of Mozart. It is easier
to understand why our works of art have a drawn, set
look and why they collapse so suddenly. It is obvious
why we have more journalists than creative writers,
more boy-scouts of painting than Cézannes, and why
sentimental tales or detective novels have taken the
place of *War and Peace* or *The Charterhouse of Parma*.
Of course, one can always meet that state of things with
a humanistic lamentation and become what Stepan

Trofimovich in *The Possessed* insists upon being: a living reproach. One can also have, like him, attacks of patriotic melancholy. But such melancholy in no way changes reality. It is better, in my opinion, to give the era its due, since it demands this so vigorously, and calmly admit that the period of the revered master, of the artist with a camellia in his buttonhole, of the armchair genius is over. To create today is to create dangerously. Any publication is an act, and that act exposes one to the passions of an age that forgives nothing. Hence the question is not to find out if this is or is not prejudicial to art. The question, for all those who cannot live without art and what it signifies, is merely to find out how, among the police forces of so many ideologies (how many churches, what solitude!), the strange liberty of creation is possible.

It is not enough to say in this regard that art is threatened by the powers of the State. If that were true, the problem would be simple: the artist fights or capitulates. The problem is more complex, more serious too, as soon as it becomes apparent that the battle is waged within the artist himself. The hatred for art, of which our society provides such fine examples, is so effective today only because it is kept alive by artists themselves. The doubt felt by the artists who preceded us concerned their own talent. The doubt felt by artists of today concerns the necessity of their art, hence their very existence. Racine in 1957 would make excuses for writing *Bérénice* when he might have been fighting to defend the Edict of Nantes.

That questioning of art by the artist has many reasons,

and only the loftiest need be considered. Among the best explanations is the feeling the contemporary artist has of lying or of indulging in useless words if he pays no attention to history's woes. What characterizes our time, indeed, is the way the masses and their wretched condition have burst upon contemporary sensibilities. We now know that they exist, whereas we once had a tendency to forget them. And if we are more aware, it is not because our aristocracy, artistic or otherwise, has become better—no, have no fear—it is because the masses have become stronger and keep people from forgetting them.

There are still other reasons, and some of them less noble, for this surrender of the artist. But, whatever those reasons may be, they all work toward the same end: to discourage free creation by undermining its basic principle, the creator's faith in himself. "A man's obedience to his own genius," Emerson said magnificently, "is faith in its purest form." And another American writer of the nineteenth century added: "So long as a man is faithful to himself, everything is in his favor, government, society, the very sun, moon, and stars." Such amazing optimism seems dead today. In most cases the artist is ashamed of himself and his privileges, if he has any. He must first of all answer the question he has put to himself: is art a deceptive luxury?

I

The first straightforward reply that can be made is this: on occasion art may be a deceptive luxury. On the poop deck of slave galleys it is possible, at any time and place, as we know, to sing of the constellations while the convicts bend over the oars and exhaust themselves in the hold; it is always possible to record the social conversation that takes place on the benches of the amphitheater while the lion is crunching the victim. And it is very hard to make any objections to the art that has known such success in the past. But things have changed somewhat, and the number of convicts and martyrs has increased amazingly over the surface of the globe. In the face of so much suffering, if art insists on being a luxury, it will also be a lie.

Of what could art speak, indeed? If it adapts itself to what the majority of our society wants, art will be a meaningless recreation. If it blindly rejects that society, if the artist makes up his mind to take refuge in his dream, art will express nothing but a negation. In this way we shall have the production of entertainers or of formal grammarians, and in both cases this leads to an art cut off from living reality. For about a century we have been living in a society that is not even the society of money (gold can arouse carnal passions) but that of the abstract symbols of money. The society of merchants can be defined as a society in which things disappear in favor of signs. When a ruling class measures its fortunes, not by the acre of land or the ingot of gold, but by the number of figures corresponding ideally to a certain number of exchange operations, it thereby condemns itself to setting a certain kind of humbug at the center of its experience and its universe. A society founded on signs is, in its essence, an artificial society in which man's carnal truth is handled as something artificial. There is no reason for being surprised that such a society chose as its religion a moral code of formal principles and that it inscribes the words "liberty" and "equality" on its prisons as well as on its temples of finance. However, words cannot be prostituted with impunity. The most misrepresented value today is certainly the value of liberty. Good minds (I have always thought there were two kinds of intelligence—intelligent intelligence and stupid intelligence) teach that it is but an obstacle on the path of true progress. But such solemn stupidities were uttered because for a hundred years a society of merchants made an exclusive and unilateral use of liberty, looking upon it as a right rather than as a duty, and did not fear to use an ideal liberty, as often as it could, to justify a very real oppression. As a result, is there anything surprising in the fact that such a society asked art to be, not an instrument of liberation, but an inconsequential exercise and a mere entertainment? Consequently, a fashionable society in which all troubles were money troubles and all worries were sentimental worries was satisfied for decades with its society novelists and with the most futile art in the world, the one about which Oscar Wilde, thinking of himself before he knew prison, said that the greatest of all vices was superficiality.

In this way the manufacturers of art (I did not say the artists) of middle-class Europe, before and after 1900, accepted irresponsibility because responsibility presupposed a painful break with their society (those who really broke with it are named Rimbaud, Nietzsche,

Strindberg, and we know the price they paid). From that period we get the theory of art for art's sake, which is merely a voicing of that irresponsibility. Art for art's sake, the entertainment of a solitary artist, is indeed the artificial art of a factitious and self-absorbed society. The logical result of such a theory is the art of little cliques or the purely formal art fed on affectations and abstractions and ending in the destruction of all reality. In this way a few works charm a few individuals while many coarse inventions corrupt many others. Finally art takes shape outside of society and cuts itself off from its living roots. Gradually the artist, even if he is celebrated, is alone or at least is known to his nation only through the intermediary of the popular press or the radio, which will provide a convenient and simplified idea of him. The more art specializes, in fact, the more necessary popularization becomes. In this way millions of people will have the feeling of knowing this or that great artist of our time because they have learned from the newspapers that he raises canaries or that he never stays married more than six months. The greatest renown today consists in being admired or hated without having been read. Any artist who goes in for being famous in our society must know that it is not he who will become famous, but someone else under his name, someone who will eventually escape him and perhaps someday will kill the true artist in him.

Consequently, there is nothing surprising in the fact that almost everything worth while created in the mercantile Europe of the nineteenth and twentieth centuries —in literature, for instance—was raised up against the society of its time. It may be said that until almost the time of the French Revolution current literature was, in the main, a literature of consent. From the moment when middle-class society, a result of the revolution, became stabilized, a literature of revolt developed instead. Official values were negated, in France, for example, either by the bearers of revolutionary values, from the Romantics to Rimbaud, or by the maintainers of aristocratic values, of whom Vigny and Balzac are good examples. In both cases the masses and the aristocracy—the two sources of all civilization—took their stand against the artificial society of their time.

But this negation, maintained so long that it is now rigid, has become artificial too and leads to another sort of sterility. The theme of the exceptional poet born into a mercantile society (Vigny's *Chatterton* is the finest example) has hardened into a presumption that one can be a great artist only against the society of one's time, whatever it may be. Legitimate in the beginning when asserting that a true artist could not compromise with the world of money, the principle became false with the subsidiary belief that an artist could assert himself only by being against everything in general. Consequently, many of our artists long to be exceptional, feel guilty if they are not, and wish for simultaneous applause and hisses. Naturally, society, tired or indifferent at present, applauds and hisses only at random. Consequently, the intellectual of today is always bracing himself stiffly to add to his height. But as a result of rejecting everything, even the tradition of his art, the contemporary artist gets the illusion that he is creating his own rule and even-

tually takes himself for God. At the same time he thinks
he can create his reality himself. But, cut off from his
society, he will create nothing but formal or abstract
works, thrilling as experiences but devoid of the fecundity we associate with true art, which is called upon to
unite. In short, there will be as much difference between the contemporary subtleties or abstractions and
the work of a Tolstoy or a Molière as between an antici-
patory draft on invisible wheat and the rich soil of the
furrow itself.

II

In this way art may be a deceptive luxury. It is not
surprising, then, that men or artists wanted to call a halt
and go back to truth. As soon as they did, they denied
that the artist had a right to solitude and offered him as a
subject, not his dreams, but reality as it is lived and en-
dured by all. Convinced that art for art's sake, through
its subjects and through its style, is not understandable to
the masses or else in no way expresses their truth, these
men wanted the artist instead to speak intentionally
about and for the majority. He has only to translate the
sufferings and happiness of all into the language of all
and he will be universally understood. As a reward for
being absolutely faithful to reality, he will achieve
complete communication among men.

This ideal of universal communication is indeed the
ideal of any great artist. Contrary to the current presumption, if there is any man who has no right to solitude, it
is the artist. Art cannot be a monologue. When the most

solitary and least famous artist appeals to posterity, he is merely reaffirming his fundamental vocation. Considering a dialogue with deaf or inattentive contemporaries to be impossible, he appeals to a more far-reaching dialogue with the generations to come.

But in order to speak about all and to all, one has to speak of what all know and of the reality common to us all. The sea, rains, necessity, desire, the struggle against death—these are the things that unite us all. We resemble one another in what we see together, in what we suffer together. Dreams change from individual to individual, but the reality of the world is common to us all. Striving toward realism is therefore legitimate, for it is basically related to the artistic adventure.

So let's be realistic. Or, rather, let's try to be so, if this is possible. For it is not certain that the word has a meaning; it is not certain that realism, even if it is desirable, is possible. Let us stop and inquire first of all if pure realism is possible in art. If we believe the declarations of the nineteenth-century naturalists, it is the exact reproduction of reality. Therefore it is to art what photography is to painting: the former reproduces and the latter selects. But what does it reproduce and what is reality? Even the best of photographs, after all, is not a sufficiently faithful reproduction, is not yet sufficiently realistic. What is there more real, for instance, in our universe than a man's life, and how can we hope to preserve it better than in a realistic film? But under what conditions is such a film possible? Under purely imaginary conditions. We should have to presuppose, in fact, an ideal camera focused on the man day and night and

constantly registering his every move. The very projec-
tion of such a film would last a lifetime and could be
seen only by an audience of people willing to waste
their lives in watching someone else's life in great detail. Even under such conditions, such an unimaginable
film would not be realistic for the simple reason that the
reality of a man's life is not limited to the spot in which
he happens to be. It lies also in other lives that give
shape to his—lives of people he loves, to begin with,
which would have to be filmed too, and also lives of
unknown people, influential and insignificant, fellow
citizens, policemen, professors, invisible comrades
from the mines and foundries, diplomats and dictators,
religious reformers, artists who create myths that are
decisive for our conduct—humble representatives, in
short, of the sovereign chance that dominates the most
routine existences. Consequently, there is but one possible realistic film: the one that is constantly shown us
by an invisible camera on the world's screen. The only
realistic artist, then, is God, if he exists. All other
artists are, *ipso facto*, unfaithful to reality.

As a result, the artists who reject bourgeois society
and its formal art, who insist on speaking of reality,
and reality alone, are caught in a painful dilemma.
They must be realistic and yet cannot be. They want to
make their art subservient to reality, and reality cannot
be described without effecting a choice that makes
it subservient to the originality of an art. The beautiful
and tragic production of the early years of the Russian
Revolution clearly illustrates this torment. What Russia
gave us then with Blok and the great Pasternak, Maia-

kovski and Essenine, Eisenstein and the first novelists of
cement and steel, was a splendid laboratory of forms and
themes, a fecund unrest, a wild enthusiasm for research.
Yet it was necessary to conclude and to tell how it was
possible to be realistic even though complete realism was
impossible. Dictatorship, in this case as in others, went
straight to the point: in its opinion realism was first
necessary and then possible so long as it was deliberately
socialistic. What is the meaning of this decree?

As a matter of fact, such a decree frankly admits that
reality cannot be reproduced without exercising a selection, and it rejects the theory of realism as it was for-
mulated in the nineteenth century. The only thing
needed, then, is to find a principle of choice that will
give shape to the world. And such a principle is found,
not in the reality we know, but in the reality that will be
—in short, the future. In order to reproduce properly
what is, one must depict also what will be. In other
words, the true object of socialistic realism is precisely
what has no reality yet

The contradiction is rather beautiful. But, after all,
the very expression of socialistic realism was contradictory. How, indeed, is a socialistic realism possible when
reality is not altogether socialistic? It is not socialistic,
for example, either in the past or altogether in the
present. The answer is easy: we shall choose in the
reality of today or of yesterday what announces and
serves the perfect city of the future. So we shall devote
ourselves, on the one hand, to negating and condemning
whatever aspects of reality are not socialistic and, on the
other hand, to glorifying what is or will become so. We
shall inevitably get a propaganda art with its heroes and

its villains—an edifying literature, in other words, just as remote as formalistic art is from complex and living reality. Finally, that art will be socialistic insofar as it is not realistic.

This aesthetic that intended to be realistic therefore becomes a new idealism, just as sterile for the true artist as bourgeois idealism. Reality is ostensibly granted a sovereign position only to be more readily thrown out. Art is reduced to nothing. It serves and, by serving, becomes a slave. Only those who keep from describing reality will be praised as realists. The others will be censured, with the approval of the former. Renown, which in bourgeois society consisted in not being read or in being misunderstood, will in a totalitarian society consist in keeping others from being read. Once more, true art will be distorted or gagged and universal communication will be made impossible by the very people who most passionately wanted it.

The easiest thing, when faced with such a defeat, would be to admit that so-called socialistic realism has little connection with great art and that the revolutionaries, in the very interest of the revolution, ought to look for another aesthetic. But it is well known that the defenders of the theory described shout that no art is possible outside it. They spend their time shouting this. But my deep-rooted conviction is that they do not believe it and that they have decided, in their hearts, that artistic values must be subordinated to the values of revolutionary action. If this were clearly stated, the discussion would be easier. One can respect such great renunciation on the part of men who suffer too much from the contrast between the unhappiness of all and the privileges sometimes associated with an artist's lot, who reject the unbearable distance separating those whom poverty gags and those whose vocation is rather to express themselves constantly. One might then understand such men, try to carry on a dialogue with them, attempt to tell them, for instance, that suppressing creative liberty is perhaps not the right way to overcome slavery and that until they can speak for all it is stupid to give up the ability to speak for a few at least. Yes, socialistic realism ought to own up to the fact that it is the twin brother of political realism. It sacrifices art for an end that is alien to art but that, in the scale of values, may seem to rank higher. In short, it suppresses art temporarily in order to establish justice first. When justice exists, in a still indeterminate future, art will resuscitate. In this way the golden rule of contemporary intelligence is applied to matters of art—the rule that insists on the impossibility of making an omelet without breaking eggs. But such overwhelming common sense must not mislead us. To make a good omelet it is not enough to break thousands of eggs, and the value of a cook is not judged, I believe, by the number of broken eggshells. If the artistic cooks of our time upset more baskets of eggs than they intended, the omelet of civilization may never again come out right, and art may never resuscitate. Barbarism is never temporary. Sufficient allowance is never made for it, and, quite naturally, from art barbarism extends to morals. Then the suffering and blood of men give birth to insignificant literatures, an ever indulgent press, photographed portraits, and sodality plays in which hatred takes the place of religion. Art culminates thus in forced optimism, the worst of luxuries, it so happens, and the most ridiculous of lies.

How could we be surprised? The suffering of mankind is such a vast subject that it seems no one could touch it unless he was like Keats so sensitive, it is said, that he could have touched pain itself with his hands. This is clearly seen when a controlled literature tries to alleviate that suffering with official consolations. The lie of art for art's sake pretended to know nothing of evil and consequently assumed responsibility for it. But the realistic lie, even though managing to admit mankind's present unhappiness, betrays that unhappiness just as seriously by making use of it to glorify a future state of happiness, about which no one knows anything, so that the future authorizes every kind of humbug.

The two aesthetics that have long stood opposed to each other, the one that recommends a complete rejection of real life and the one that claims to reject anything that is not real life, end up, however, by coming to agreement, far from reality, in a single lie and in the suppression of art. The academicism of the Right does not even acknowledge a misery that the academicism of the Left utilizes for ulterior reasons. But in both cases the misery is only strengthened at the same time that art is negated.

III

Must we conclude that this lie is the very essence of art? I shall say instead that the attitudes I have been describing are lies only insofar as they have but little relation to art. What, then, is art? Nothing simple, that is certain. And it is even harder to find out amid the shouts of so many people bent on simplifying everything. On the one hand, genius is expected to be splendid and solitary; on the other hand, it is called upon to resemble all. Alas, reality is more complex. And Balzac suggested this in a sentence: "The genius resembles everyone and no one resembles him." So it is with art, which is nothing without reality and without which reality is insignificant. How, indeed, could art get along without the real and how could art be subservient to it? The artist chooses his object as much as he is chosen by it. Art, in a sense, is a revolt against everything fleeting and unfinished in the world. Consequently, its only aim is to give another form to a reality that it is nevertheless forced to preserve as the source of its emotion. In this regard, we are all realistic and no one is. Art is neither complete rejection nor complete acceptance of what is. It is simultaneously rejection and acceptance, and this is why it must be a perpetually renewed wrenching apart. The artist constantly lives in such a state of ambiguity, incapable of negating the real and yet eternally bound to question it in its eternally unfinished aspects. In order to paint a still life, there must be confrontation and mutual adjustment between a painter and an apple. And if forms are nothing without the world's lighting, they in turn add to that lighting. The real universe which, by its radiance, calls forth bodies and statues receives from them at the same time a second light that determines the light from the sky. Consequently, great style lies midway between the artist and his object.

There is no need of determining whether art must flee reality or defer to it, but rather what precise dose of reality the work must take on as ballast to keep from floating up among the clouds or from dragging along the ground with weighted boots. Each artist solves this problem according to his lights and abilities. The greater an artist's revolt against the world's reality, the greater can be the weight of reality to balance that revolt. But the weight can never stifle the artist's solitary exigency. The loftiest work will always be, as in the Greek tragedians, Melville, Tolstoy, or Molière, the work that maintains an equilibrium between reality and man's rejection of that reality, each forcing the other upward in a ceaseless overflowing, characteristic of life itself at its most joyous and heart-rending extremes. Then, every once in a while, a new world appears, different from the everyday world and yet the same, particular but universal, full of innocent insecurity—called forth for a few hours by the power and longing of genius. That's just it and yet that's not it; the world is nothing and the world is everything—this is the contradictory and tireless cry of every true artist, the cry that keeps him on his feet with eyes ever open and that, every once in a while, awakens for all in this world asleep the fleeting and insistent image of a reality we recognize without ever having known it.

Likewise, the artist can neither turn away from his time nor lose himself in it. If he turns away from it, he speaks in a void. But, conversely, insofar as he takes his time as his object, he asserts his own existence as subject and cannot give in to it altogether. In other words, at the very moment when the artist chooses to share the fate of all, he asserts the individual he is. And he cannot escape from this ambiguity. The artist takes from history what he can see of it himself or undergo himself, directly or indirectly—the immediate event, in other words, and men who are alive today, not the relationship of that immediate event to a future that is invisible to the living artist. Judging contemporary man in the name of a man who does not yet exist is the function of prophecy. But the artist can value the myths that are offered him only in relation to their repercussion on living people. The prophet, whether religious or political, can judge absolutely and, as is known, is not chary of doing so. But the artist cannot. If he judged absolutely, he would arbitrarily divide reality into good and evil and thus indulge in melodrama. The aim of art, on the contrary, is not to legislate or to reign supreme, but rather to understand first of all. Sometimes it does reign supreme, as a result of understanding. But no work of genius has ever been based on hatred and contempt. This is why the artist, at the end of his slow advance, absolves instead of condemning. Instead of being a judge, he is a justifier. He is the perpetual advocate of the living creature, because it is alive. He truly argues for love of one's neighbor and not for that love of the remote stranger which debases contemporary humanism until it becomes the catechism of the law court. Instead, the great work eventually confounds all judges. With it the artist simultaneously pays homage to the loftiest figure of mankind and bows down before the worst of criminals. "There is not," Wilde wrote in prison, "a single wretched man in this wretched place along with me who does not stand in symbolic relation to the very secret of life." Yes, and that secret of life coincides with the secret of art.

For a hundred and fifty years the writers belonging to a mercantile society, with but few exceptions, thought they could live in happy irresponsibility. They lived, indeed, and then died alone, as they had lived. But we writers of the twentieth century shall never again be alone. Rather, we must know that we can never escape the common misery and that our only justification, if indeed there is a justification, is to speak up, insofar as we can, for those who cannot do so. But we must do so for all those who are suffering at this moment, whatever may be the glories, past or future, of the States and parties oppressing them: for the artist there are no privileged torturers. This is why beauty, even today, especially today, cannot serve any party; it cannot serve, in the long or short run, anything but men's suffering or their liberty. The only really committed artist is he who, without refusing to take part in the combat, at least refuses to join the regular armies and remains a free-lance. The lesson he then finds in beauty, if he draws it fairly, is a lesson not of selfishness but rather of hard brotherhood. Looked upon thus, beauty has never enslaved anyone. And for thousands of years, every day, at every second, it has instead assuaged the servitude of millions of men and, occasionally, liberated some of them once and for all. After all, perhaps the greatness of art lies in the perpetual tension between beauty and pain, the love of men and the madness of creation, unbearable solitude and the exhausting crowd, rejection and consent. Art advances between two chasms, which are frivolity and propaganda. On the ridge where the great artist moves forward, every step is an adventure, an extreme risk. In that risk, however, and only there, lies the freedom of art. A difficult freedom that is more like an ascetic discipline? What artist would deny this? What artist would dare to claim that he was equal to such a ceaseless task? Such freedom presupposes health of body and mind, a style that reflects strength of soul, and a patient defiance. Like all freedom, it is a perpetual risk, an exhausting adventure, and this is why people avoid the risk today, as they avoid liberty with its exacting demands, in order to accept any kind of bondage and achieve at least comfort of soul. But if art is not an adventure, what is it and where is its justification? No, the free artist is no more a man of comfort than is the free man. The free artist is the one who, with great effort, creates his own order. The more undisciplined what he must put in order, the stricter will be his rule and the more he will assert his freedom. There is a remark of Gide that I have always approved although it may be easily misunderstood: "Art lives on constraint and dies of freedom." That is true. But it must not be interpreted as meaning that art can be controlled. Art lives only on the constraints it imposes on itself; it dies of all others. Conversely, if it does not constrain itself, it indulges in ravings and becomes a slave to mere shadows. The freest art and the most rebellious will therefore be the most classical; it will reward the greatest effort. So long as a society and its artists do not accept this long and free effort, so long as they relax in the comfort of amusements or the comfort of conformism, in the games of art for art's sake or the preachings of realistic art, its artists are lost in nihilism and sterility. Saying this amounts to saying that today the rebirth depends on our courage and our will to be lucid.

Yes, the rebirth is in the hands of all of us. It is up to us if the West is to bring forth any anti-Alexanders to tie together the Gordian Knot of civilization cut by the sword. For this purpose, we must assume all the risks and labors of freedom. There is no need of knowing whether, by pursuing justice, we shall manage to preserve liberty. It is essential to know that, without liberty, we shall achieve nothing and that we shall lose both future justice and ancient beauty. Liberty alone draws men from their isolation; but slavery dominates a crowd of solitudes. And art, by virtue of that free essence I have tried to define, unites whereas tyranny separates. It is not surprising, therefore, that art should be the enemy marked out by every form of oppression. It is not surprising that artists and intellectuals should have been the first victims of modern tyrannies, whether of the Right or of the Left. Tyrants know there is in the work of art an emancipatory force, which is mysterious only to those who do not revere it. Every great work makes the human face more admirable and richer, and this is its whole secret. And thousands of concentration camps and barred cells are not enough to hide this staggering testimony of dignity. This is why it is not true that culture can be, even temporarily, suspended in order to make way for a new culture. Man's unbroken testimony as to his suffering and his nobility cannot be suspended; the act of breathing cannot be suspended. There is no culture without legacy, and we cannot and must not reject anything of ours, the legacy of the West. Whatever the works of the future may be, they will bear the same secret, made up of courage and freedom, nourished by the daring of thousands of artists of all times and all nations. Yes, when modern tyranny shows us that, even when confined to his calling, the artist is a public enemy, it is right. But in this way tyranny pays its respects, through the artist, to an image of man that nothing has ever been able to crush.

My conclusion will be simple. It will consist of saying, in the very midst of the sound and the fury of our history: "Let us rejoice." Let us rejoice, indeed, at having witnessed the death of a lying and comfort-loving Europe and at being faced with cruel truths. Let us rejoice as men because a prolonged hoax has collapsed and we see clearly what threatens us. And let us rejoice as artists, torn from our sleep and our deafness, forced to keep our eyes on destitution, prisons, and bloodshed. If, faced with such a vision, we can preserve the memory of days and of faces, and if, conversely, faced with the world's beauty, we manage not to forget the humiliated, then Western art will gradually recover its strength and its sovereignty. To be sure, there are few examples in history of artists confronted with such hard problems. But when even the simplest words and phrases cost their weight in freedom and blood, the artist must learn to handle them with restraint. Danger makes men classical, and all greatness, after all, is rooted in risk.

The time of irresponsible artists is over. We shall regret it for our little moments of bliss. But we shall be able to admit that this ordeal contributes meanwhile to our chances of authenticity, and we shall accept the challenge. The freedom of art is not worth much when its only purpose is to assure the artist's comfort. For a value or a virtue to take root in a society, there must be no lying about it; in other words, we must pay for it every time we can. If liberty has become dangerous, then it may cease to be prostituted. And I cannot agree, for example, with those who complain today of the decline of wisdom. Apparently they are right. Yet, to tell the truth, wisdom has never declined so much as when it involved no risks and belonged exclusively to a few humanists buried in libraries. But today, when at last it has to face real dangers, there is a chance that it may again stand up and be respected.

It is said that Nietzsche after the break with Lou Salomé, in a period of complete solitude, crushed and uplifted at the same time by the perspective of the huge work he had to carry on without any help, used to walk at night on the mountains overlooking the gulf of Genoa and light great bonfires of leaves and branches which he would watch as they burned. I have often dreamed of those fires and have occasionally imagined certain men and certain works in front of those fires, as a way of testing men and works. Well, our era is one of those fires whose unbearable heat will doubtless reduce many a work to ashes! But as for those which remain, their metal will be intact, and, looking at them, we shall be able to indulge without restraint in the supreme joy of the intelligence which we call "admiration."

One may long, as I do, for a gentler flame, a respite, a pause for musing. But perhaps there is no other peace for the artist than what he finds in the heat of combat. "Every wall is a door," Emerson correctly said. Let us not look for the door, and the way out, anywhere but in the wall against which we are living. Instead, let us seek the respite where it is—in the very thick of the battle. For in my opinion, and this is where I shall close, it *is* there. Great ideas, it has been said, come into the world as gently as doves. Perhaps then, if we listen attentively, we shall hear, amid the uproar of empires and nations, a faint flutter of wings, the gentle stirring of life and hope. Some will say that this hope lies in a nation; others, in a man. I believe rather that it is awakened, revived, nourished by millions of solitary individuals whose deeds and works every day negate frontiers and the crudest implications of history. As a result, there shines forth fleetingly the ever threatened truth that each and every man, on the foundation of his own sufferings and joys, builds for all.

A NOTE ABOUT THE AUTHOR

ALBERT CAMUS was born in Mondovi, Algeria, in 1913 of peasant stock and was brought up in a poor suburb of Algiers. He worked his way through school and university, writing a thesis in philosophy while dividing his spare time between rugby and a theatrical stock company he organized. He had overcome a serious threat of tuberculosis and before he was twenty had begun writing essays and stories. Then journalism took him to the French mainland.

In occupied France of 1942 he published *The Myth of Sisyphus* and *The Stranger,* a philosophical essay and a novel that first brought him to the attention of intellectual circles. But after the Liberation the public learned that the young author of these books had meanwhile been fighting in the underground and it was he who was responsible for the celebrated editorials that appeared in the clandestine paper *Combat.*

Camus continued to distinguish himself with three widely praised works of fiction—*The Plague, The Fall,* and *Exile and the Kingdom,* with his essay *The Rebel* and three published volumes of *Actuelles,* and with his writing for the theater, which included *Caligula and Three Other Plays* and his adaptation of Dostoevsky's *The Possessed.* The official citation accompanying the 1957 Nobel Prize for Literature said that Camus was awarded this highest international honor because of "his important literary production, which with clearsighted earnestness illuminates the problems of the human conscience in our times."

On January 4, 1960, Albert Camus was killed in an automobile accident.

December 1960